MAY
TOMORROW
BE AWAKE

MAY TOMORROW BE AWAKE

ON POETRY, AUTISM, AND OUR NEURODIVERSE FUTURE

Chris Martin

HarperOne
An Imprint of HarperCollins*Publishers*

Names and identifying characteristics of some individuals have been changed.

Grateful acknowledgment is given to the following for the use of their work in this publication:

"I Use Patterns to Survive," "Awed," "A Volcano Named Eati," "Parenting During a Quarantine," and "May," © Max and Mark Eati. Used by permission.

"The Maker of Wanting Space," "Isolation Song of Love," "Calm-Arriving to a Wanting Safe World," "Owls Easy on the Ways of Language," and "Tall Ideas," © Adam Wolfond. Used by permission.

"He Hears," © Bill Bernard. Used by permission.

"Hannah Is Never Only Hannah," "The Listening World," "Animal Ear," "Between," "Becoming Mud," "How the World Began," and "The Underworld," © Hannah Emerson. Used by permission.

"Thirteen Ways of Looking at Dwight D. Eisenhower," © Max Zolotukhin-Ridgway. Used by permission.

"All About Me," "Feeling Rich," "Rainbow Man," "Rainbow Man Enters the Ring," "My Life," "All the Things Chris Doesn't Know," "They Break You Down," and "Ode," © Lonnie Shaw. Used by permission.

"In the Quarantine Body" and "Have Hidden Great Hibernating Truths," © Imane Boukaila. Used by permission.

"Tuning Goes Frig," "Rotary Club," "I No a Poet," and "Mud," © Sid Ghosh. Used by permission.

"we are other together," © Amelia Bell. Used by permission.

HarperCollins books may be purchased for educational, business, or sales promotional use. For information, please email the Special Markets Department at SPsales@harpercollins.com.

FIRST EDITION

Designed by Elina Cohen

Library of Congress Cataloging-in-Publication Data has been applied for.

ISBN 978-0-06-302015-3

22 23 24 25 26   LSC   10 9 8 7 6 5 4 3 2 1

For Mark, Max, Adam, Matteo, Hannah, Imane, Zach,
Bill, Khalil, Lonnie, Soren, Dustin, Wallace, Brian,
Amelia, Brother Sid, and Rowan

This is what I want to do. This is what I want to be, surrounded by kindred spirits, doing useful things with care, knowledge and clarity.

—Dara McAnulty, *Diary of a Young Naturalist*

Take good care
to shape with language
worlds that want to hold us all

—Adjua Gargi Nzinga Greaves,
Of Forests and of Farms: On Faculty and Failure

CONTENTS

MAY
TOMORROW
BE AWAKE

Keepers of the Light

The Rallying Dance—To Extend the Choreography—
Forging a Whetstone—To Educate Myself—Angling Toward
Autonomy—Denizens of the Intense World—The Lava of
Language—To Reach and Root—The Light That Leaps Forth

I watch from my end of the video chat as Adam's lanky frame once again escapes the purview of my Zoom screen. He is answering the beckoning call of a stick he gleaned from the woods earlier that day. When Estée, his mother and communication partner, reorients their screen in Toronto, I can see Adam rhythmically twallowing[1] the stick in his left hand, expertly moving it back and forth like a windshield wiper or wing. Estée takes the keyboard to him and Adam begins typing again with his right hand: "I am wanting to ask you a question I have. I am wanting to ask the teacher how you can think with me so easily about doing poetry love that you can have thinking about much movement using me good to have support about it and understanding. That is meaningful to me and I thank you doing the dance."

This dance—which Adam alternatively calls a jam or an assembly or a rally—was at once metaphorical and real. Adam, who is a nonspeaking autistic eighteen-year-old, often makes a peripatetic sort of dance of our one-hour session, alternately typing and repositioning himself elsewhere in the room. But he also leads the dance of conversation by way of his writing, which sets a different choreography in motion. Today, as most days, the three of us are joined by Ellen, one of Adam's art collaborators. Like Adam, Ellen and Estée are both artists who often work in material or sculptural modes. But sculpture, writing, dancing, twallowing: these forms all stay in conversation when we're with Adam. In between his sustained waves of typing, which sometimes last for a hundred words or more, only punctuated by the spaces that separate them, he pauses to replenish himself and welcomes reflections on what he's just written. Or just as often a reflection on *how* he's just written, as together we revel in the patterns of sound and sense Adam is drawing forth.

Our ideas as writers and artists bring us into a thrilling intellectual tango, which happens alongside the tactile dance of Adam's fingers on the keys. As Adam types, I take the words down in a shared Google Doc. As his fluid sentences emerge, voiced one word at a time by the vocal synthesizer connected to his iPad, my mind attempts to keep pace and my heart leaps to think in this way, doing the "poetry love" that brings us all into a swell of fellow feeling. It is in these swells and waves that we continuously welcome each other into the ongoing dance of collaboration, interdependence, and neurodiversity.[2]

"Poetry love" can be a hard thing to explain to people who are not in the practice of it, people who have often been alienated from the possibilities of it by their previous experiences, most commonly the experiences they had in high school. Poetry is an art form that can be difficult to pin down, and when people try too hard to pin it down, they often ruin everything that makes poetry magical. When you focus on what poetry *is*, or worse, *should* be, you instantly lose the most important thing about the practice of making a poem: what *could* be. What could and can and does happen in a poem is the light at the heart of its practice. If the poet uses constraints or rules or restrictive patterns in a poem, it is always to open up something larger: a feeling, an experience, a connection.

And if it's hard to explain poetry, it would seem even more difficult to explain the remarkable reciprocity poetry shares with autism or autistic minds or autistic ways of moving through the world. Is it the way patterns—rhyme, line count, meter—so crucially embed themselves into the visual and sonic framework of each poem? Do the poem's formal elements—line breaks, stanzas, repetitions—delineate a space where creative decisions are more readily perceived and undertaken? Is there an almost architectural element to building poems that lets autistic writers inhabit their particular ways of making language? Does the hand of the poem open to the writer (and reader) in a way that leaves space for the breadth and depth of autistic intensity? Whatever it is, I have watched my students, time and again, grasp the hand of poetry and begin dancing like they've been doing it their whole lives.

It's my pleasure to welcome you into the dance also—the dance that's all so thrillingly expanding around us as we move into a future characterized by movement. I write these words on the winter solstice of 2020, at a time when cultural and political movements have unveiled so much of the destructive machinery that treats certain bodies as negligible, silenceable, and disposable. I am writing from Minneapolis, where the murder of George Floyd, ten minutes away from my house, led to global uprising, an emergent movement that seeks accountability, reckoning, and a pathway to liberation. These movements resonate alongside the neurodiversity movement, which is changing the way that we understand cognitive and sensorimotor difference, shifting us away from a pathology model, where people are judged by how "independently" they can hew to some unknown quantity of "normal" or "neurotypical," and toward an ethics of interdependence, where our differences allow us to support one another while finding the particular supports we each need to thrive.[3] To support and be supported in mutual, consensual measure. To find reciprocity among our neighbors. To find belonging.

For me to answer Adam's question, I would need to better understand how we belonged together. What was the source of our dance's ease? To what abundance of belonging had we mutually attuned? In the moment, I said something about our shared love of patterns and language, of what Adam calls "languaging." And of course I thanked him for inviting me into the rallying dance, which I also find deeply meaningful—as a teacher, but also as a poet and as a friend. I thanked him for supporting me with his thoughts, which helped so much to clarify my own. Clarify, but also recognize. Adam's languaging always helps me to rethink my own manner of moving through the world and to recognize myself as a neurodivergent dancer, one who seeks always to "extend the choreography," as Adam has written. To put it another way, the work I do tends to remind me of who I am.

This kind of self-recognition has been hard-won. I was born near the end of a violent decade near the end of a violent century near the end of a violent millennium. And I was born into a body that resembled the bodies of those who have historically wielded the most power with the most violence toward the most oppressive ends. I am a White male who can selectively pass as cis, straight, able, and neurotypical. This is what Sonya Renee Taylor calls "the default body," and its cover has given me tremendous advantages, including the ability to move through a neurotypical world with something approximating ease.[4] But this false ease is nothing like what I feel when Adam and I are in conversation. The truth is that I have never felt like I belonged in the neurotypical world, much less amidst the callous materialism and masculinity that seek ever to make me complicit in their conditioning. The truth is that I now question all these aspects of my identity, desiring to know where the enforcement of normativity ends and I begin.

I don't recall the first time I was called *sensitive*, but as a child the word seemed always sewn onto my shirt pocket like an invisible name tag. I wasn't an overtly emotional child, but that didn't stop teachers, family friends, or even strangers from picking up on it instantly: Christopher is very *sensitive*, isn't he?[5] As the adjective predictably spilled from their lips, their faces angled in concern, I could tell it was meant to both flatter and fret. It was a gift, this sensitivity, something that distinguished me from others, but it was also, I inferred, a source of vulnerability, especially for a boy. As I prepared to move to New York City in my early twenties, a seasoned writer warned me, "You're *sensitive* Chris, the city will eat you alive."[6]

We didn't have words like "neurodivergent" in the 1980s, especially not in Colorado Springs, but I had the great fortune of being raised by two very successful neurodivergent parents. My dyslexic father was a nationally recognized bankruptcy lawyer, and my mother, despite an undiagnosed attentional disorder, was a keen social worker who cofounded what is now the longest running women-focused film festival in the world. Looking back, I can see clearly that the neurodivergent parts of their personalities were not what held them back, but what made them extraordinary.

Their sensitive son was also extraordinary, what we'd now call "twice-exceptional," the kind of student who struggles and excels in equal measure, often to the consternation of their teachers. When I wasn't sitting on the dreaded green bench outside the principal's office, having again disrupted class with my unwieldy and exuberant body, I was exceeding all my academic benchmarks. Ms. Johnson, my second grade teacher and an early champion, routinely had to demand my attention because I was singing aloud at my desk without realizing it. We made a compromise: after I sped through the weekly math test, I could head directly to the library, where I'd spend the rest of the period tracing maps and drawing wolfmen. I could sense some things easily, like intuitive ways to solve problems, but I couldn't seem to register or regulate my own relentless energy. I was confident, unwary, buzzing and bounding through the world like a big blond bee seeking pollen. Looking back, I have to imagine how my experience of school (and the world) would have been different if I hadn't had the cultural insulation of whiteness and its "boys will be boys" rhetoric to protect me. As a high school senior, prompted by my mother, who would soon seek out her own diagnosis, I would officially become diagnosed with ADHD (attention-deficit/hyperactivity disorder). The diagnosis was revealing in many ways, accounting for many of the circumstances in which I didn't "fit in," but it also left me unsatisfied. And for good reason; over the years it has become clear that my atypicality is not limited to those letters alone.

I have come to foreground neurodivergence in my way of moving through the world, but in the '90s there were no positive associations with the "deficits" inherent to my "disorder," nor was there a community of support.[7] Instead, I found another label that seemed to suit how I thought and who I wanted to be in the world: *poet*. I found writing poems exceptionally difficult, and I loved it. Poems could hold all my boundless energy and, with practice, direct it toward an endless palette of linguistic opportunities. In a poem I was encouraged to do things differently, to forge the creative and unexpected pathways that were my intrinsic strength. In college I dove headlong into the world of contemporary poetry, seeking out work that signaled new expressive horizons and poets who challenged the way I thought. I had discovered a multiverse where my racing, discursive, associative intellect was channeled into buzzing focus. I felt like I could be all of who I was.[8]

While many of my peers were jumping into MFA programs with an eye toward teaching in academia, I was looking for a less obvious route. Inspired by poet-teachers like Ron Padgett, I wanted to work with younger students. I got my first chance in an after-school program at a middle school in Brooklyn, where I found myself working with a young man, named Matteo, who wanted nothing more than to explore the movie *Planet of the Apes*. The joy I took in working with Matteo, and other students whom I would later recognize as autistic, was natural. My gifts as a sensitive boy, now a man living in the epicenter of American poetry, served me well in collaborating with neurodivergent students. I listened closely and relished the creative effort of helping these unique students access their own gifts, which I found startling and self-evident.

Over time I began to discern how poetry's patterned structure uniquely serves neurodivergent thinking—and vice versa—something I'd discovered in my own creative investigations. Initially drawn to poetry because of its rhymes and rules, I soon discovered that inventing new patterns pleased me even more than recapitulating standard ones. As a baby poet living in San Francisco, having already tried sestinas and villanelles and contrapuntals and any other form I could find, I tasked myself with inventing a new poetic form every day for a year. Not to impress anyone, or attract social media attention, but simply to revel in the possibilities and deepen my understanding of what poetry can do. Even now, having published four full-length collections of poetry, I find that those patterns and constraints continue to give me a unique thrill: part tuning fork and part obstacle course, part piggyback and part three-legged race. They whisk me forward while simultaneously holding me back, creating the generative friction necessary to hone language and thought as they emerge. Patterns work to organize, challenge, and divert my words, forging a whetstone over which they can grow sharp and smooth.

Many of the writers you will meet in this book don't need to seek out constraints. When they haven't been negotiating the constraints of their own sensorimotor complexity, they have been struggling against the constraints of a society built to minimize the complexity of their intellect and expression.[9] Whether it's through staggeringly low expectations or lack of access to communication support, these students and their insights are often held back by a dam of societal neglect. I can't tell you the number of times I have sat down with a nonspeaking writer and they have begun our session with a phrase like, "I've been waiting for this" or "I am so excited you are here." Then comes the flood, even if it appears to trickle out one painstakingly typed letter at a time. When given the opportunity to express themselves creatively, I have seen nonspeaking writers summon the kind of focused stamina that puts free climbers to shame.

Which is not to say that patterns don't still serve a crucial role. In their poem "I Use Patterns to Survive," nonspeaking autist Max Eati[10] advises the reader: "Feel it and follow it." They continue:

My life follows a pattern
of many other autistics
so I learn from them

Our lives are products
of invincible codes
that create invincible patterns

I write and update them
I design and fuel them
into real life circumstances

and add simplicity
to educate myself

To feel and follow the pattern is to educate ourselves and create access points that help navigate a path forward. So many of the autists I know are autodidacts, self-taught apprehenders of the world's complex and largely unseen systems. And like so much that we do in life—for ourselves, by ourselves, outside of any school (or tuition)—this kind of self-education is largely an act of intuition. We feel our way through the flesh and texture of an abundant world toward the focus of frequency, seeking, above all else, a sense of simplicity, of attunement. Instead of memorizing facts to prepare for some uncertain future life, we become autodidacts of the now, a manifold of objects and creatures and atmospheres that call us into perception. This is the dance Adam writes about so vibrantly, a flow made possible by our abiding relation to a nearly impossible world, so bursting it is with sensory detail. Patterns help us tune in to the inherent simplicity we seek, a wayfaring line amid the spectacular chaos of contemporary life. They move us from the babbling "patter" of life, as Adam would say, to the "pattern" of it, tuning in to meaningful ways of languaging.

This practice of pattern formed the foundation of my early work as a teaching-writer. I encountered student after student thrilled by the idea of inventing poetic forms that perfectly suited their particular passions. In a workshop at the University of Arizona Poetry Center, I helped a young man elaborate his vision for a poetry of swooping, unbroken parallel lines, enabling him to write an epic tribute to telephone wires, since he liked nothing more than to draw from memory the pattern of those lines crisscrossing the desert landscape. Another time, I spoke to a teaching-artist whose client had dislocated her knee five times and now began every conversation by asking her interlocutor about their own experience with dislocations. In ten minutes, with the help of other teaching-artists in our pedagogy workshop, we brainstormed a poetic form replete with echoes of her client's fascination: a five-stanza poem wherein each stanza would feature a dislocation (using the tab key) at the exact point when a "kn" word appeared (know, knit, knuckle, knockout, and of course knee).

There are hundreds of these examples and the list is growing. When I work with schools, we often print anthologies where the "recipes" for these new forms are included so that other teachers and students can utilize them moving forward. The sonnet form will always captivate me, but for a twelve-year-old who wants nothing more than to endlessly pour over anime comics, what form could be more thrillingly relevant than an "aniME," a self-portrait that alternatively focuses on four of your favorite anime characters? Poems have the potential to tailor, fine-tune, and pattern passion into form. The forms that result establish a creative feedback loop with the content.

Formal suggestions are one way to scaffold the creative process for students, especially when they are just learning the possibilities of poetic writing or the motor technique of an AAC (alternative and augmentative communication) method or both.[11] I learned quickly that no standardized approach can satisfy the diversity of needs and abilities my students inhabit. Each student requires their own unique supports and a leading role in shaping those supports. Since we meet once a week, many students spend several of the interceding days cultivating poems internally. Other students like to begin the session with a brief conversation, discovering there the linguistic impetus for their own writing. I come to each session prepared to prompt a student in the direction of writing, but I always ask them if they have something in mind before I do. It's a dance:

forever angling toward the autonomy of the student while ensuring that they are not alone.

Once the writing begins, I am listening as closely as possible, dictating the lines into a Google Doc. For a writer like Adam, letting the writing flow and unfold without interruption is paramount. For many alternatively communicating writers, the hard-won fluidity of typing leads to sustained thinking that ranges past traditional grammatical structures. Stopping to insert punctuation would threaten the expression itself. "Correct" sentences do not capture what Adam wants to express and how he goes about it. His long lines often emerge with three or more waves of language, delineating a swerve in thought while maintaining connection to what came before. While Adam is typing, I map out these swerves, and we discuss the structure when each set of waves carried by his typing is complete. Some students prefer to break lines themselves, either while they are writing or afterward. Some students create an initial pattern that they ask me to follow as the rest of the poem emerges. If I am tasked with finding a preliminary shape for the poem, I will reflect what is happening to the student several times during the process, both to confirm that the shape fits their vision and to let their writing bend the shape to its intentions.

Some students welcome feedback on their work as they compose, while others can't entertain even a single suggestion until they feel the poem is complete, lest it tangle their process or instigate self-doubt. Sometimes my most important role as teacher is doing nothing. And doing nothing, as I've learned, can very much be doing something. The very fact of my availability, my way of being intensely present, holds open a space that the student feels sufficiently welcomed to fill. This is the hardest part to write about, because it is largely unspoken. I am actively receptive, holding one side of an invisible tether, ready to step in when a student loses focus or falls into unproductive quandary. And I am listening, always listening, ready to reflect back all the treasures a student has already spread out before us, the tools that they've given us to understand what the poem is doing and wants to do.

When the writing is ostensibly complete, I confirm that there is nothing more the student wants to add or change before we listen to the poem read aloud. This is a nearly sacred moment: all that music and rhythm and carefully patterned emphasis becoming audible for the first time. The students' smiles as they hear what they've just written is enough to melt even the most impassive teacher. And as you've probably guessed, I'm far from stoic. After gathering myself, I confirm once again that everything looks and sounds exactly right to the writer. Because I am so often transcribing what I hear from computer-generated voice over the imperfect audio of my own computer, it's crucial that we check every single word. My process with each student is necessarily different, but the way I prioritize their vision is steadfast.

These consistent integrity checks often provide an opportunity for us to discuss their poetics and better elucidate a vision for what they hope to achieve and how. Once the words are on the page, we revel and awe at the unlikeliness of it all. Not that these neurodivergent students are writing poetry, because that now seems to me like the most common thing in the world, but that a poem gets written. Every poet I know feels the poem to exist somewhere beyond them. When it's there on the page, having left the poet's determined fingers, it stands and sings on its own. That's when we can take a closer look at all the layers and movements. We are both readers in that moment, taking in whatever emergent structure the words called forth. I attempt to articulate the patterns of each poem, to acknowledge not only the inherent gift they represent to the reader, but also how the student is teaching me once again how to acknowledge their particular patterns, which together constitute a manner of entirely unique languaging that brings them joyful ease.

We all seek patterns. But neurodivergent individuals tend to seek them out with a combination of knack and urgency that is startling, and not coincidental. In 2010, Kamila and Henry Markram posited the "intense world theory," which explores the way autistic neurology is characterized by ways of processing the world that are both uniquely dynamic and uniquely complex.[12] They posited that autistic minds aren't underresourced, as was often considered to be the case, but overconnected. They noted that the "fabric" of autistic brain circuitry is much more dense and ornate than in the general population. This is one key to understanding why many young children seem to "regress" into autism around age two or three, just at the time when most young brains are beginning to prune neurons away for a more streamlined set of connections. This abundance of connectivity often leads to synesthetic experiences of the world—"hearing" colors or "tasting" sounds. But it can also create a sort of cognitive and perceptual feedback, the bandwidth too wide to be processed amid the chaos of neurotypical life. If, as intense world theory argues, we think of the autistic brain as being like a supercomputer, we can begin to understand how crucial context and environment are to the success of that processing potential. Denizens of the intense world desire a means to tune out sensory feedback and tune in the deep focus of perception, turning intensity from foe to friend.

Though it's clear that this vocabulary of processing can be useful, I also want to push back a little on the neuroreductive objectification this supercomputer metaphor can engender, for it threatens once again to obscure the essential humanness of autistic experience. My students and I relate as friends, trusting that we're each there to listen and learn, to extend kindnesses and generosities that befit our ever-evolving fellowship. So while neurological frameworks may be helpful in conceptualizing autistic cognition, teaching is something entirely different. It's two people sitting with each other, looking to connect. Watching for meaning in movement. Listening for moments in language that resonate and exhilarate.

One of my students, Sid Ghosh, a nonspeaking autist with Down syndrome, offers us a more natural metaphor for autistic intensity:

Volcanic Mind

Hummingfriends torquescrew
language into my mining

mind. Mind secretes
modes of intense

lava. Lava makes
own path. Fire forges

mind. To think mind is hot
is to hammer bones with air.

For Sid, forging mind is an intense and ongoing process, one that can be helped along by "hummingfriends" who "torque-screw" language. Tuning in allows Sid to secrete the raw material of thought, which then seeks its own paths. When I asked Sid whether the hummingfriends were birds or people, he replied, "Both." Sid hears birds and they prompt the forge of his mind. He hears humming words (hammering on his ear bones with air), as friends ask a question or read his last line aloud. After the forge is stoked and the lava of language begins to flow, this treasure may still desire a mold to pour itself into, a form that can hold its immense value in shape.

This is where poetry comes in. I believe the sensuous patterns and dynamic formal possibilities of poetry are uniquely designed to help autists translate aspects of their intense, multidimensional thought into linguistic expression. Poems carry the dynamism embodied in movement: mining, forging, hammering. Poems and patterns help organize the innate movement of the body into thought, initiating a complex dance that one of my students, Imane Boukaila, calls "motioning truth." And again, I think it's important to note that this process of motioning truth isn't unique to autists. Through routine, habit, predilection, we all summon the patterns that might help us grasp our own truths and meet the challenge of any moment. But those challenges, especially for many of my autistic students, feature a bracing combination of sensory intensity and motor perplexity that can set the world swirling. No wonder, then, that they move so often toward the anchor pattern provides.

Though these patterns arise differently for each person, there are overlaps, a confluence of ways in which we begin to find commonality. Poems can be a meeting ground where we share our complementary experiences of the world. Poems and patterns can ground us, and the commons of our overlapping ground can be a place where we grow consensual, neurodiverse futures. Or, to borrow a neologism from Hannah Emerson, another student of mine: poems are where we can "grownd." This word is born from her observation that to authentically reach—in the direction of thoughts, dreams, or connection—one must also authentically root. In her writing, Hannah creates a pattern of reaches and roots to hold her phrases, which often begin with an anaphoric "please" and end with the doubled "yes" of her joyful epistrophe. I encourage you to read this poem aloud, allowing yourself to be carried forward by its insistent repetition.

Hannah Is Never Only Hannah

Please get that I am the trying
breeze going through the really
great great great world yes yes.

Please get that I am the drowning
helpful freedom of the storm yes
yes. Please get that I am the very

hot great great great sun yes yes.
Please get that I am the great
great great great ice that gives

you the freeze that you need
to get to melt into nothing yes
yes yes yes. Please get that I

am the sky great great great blue
nothing yes yes. Please get that
I am the grownd great great great

place helping you helping you
stand in grateful helpful helpful
helpful kissing her her her her

yes. Please get that you and I
greet the great great life from this
place of great great kissing life

life life life yes yes yes. Please
get that you are great form great
formless helping kissing kissing

great knowing the great great
great helpful kissing the trying
yes yes. Please get that helpful

loving thinking you help just help
kissing helpful loving great great
great world turn upside down yes

yes. Please get that you help me
by helping me turn upside down
too yes yes yes. Please get that

great great helpful kissing people
need to get that great helpful kissing
is turning kissing upside down yes

yes. Please get that helpful kissing
just needs to be gathered into this
helpful kissing trying hell of this life

to go forward to help me Hannah
Hannah Hannah yes yes. Please
get that you need loving kissing

to make you like me yes yes.
Please get that the kissing must
be great knotting of you me great

us together in this hell yes yes yes.
Please get that you kiss me helping
me kiss you yes yes.

This wasn't the first time Hannah had used the neologism
"grownd" and so I was prepared when she spelled it that way.
I had also encountered her repetitions of "great" and "yes," as
well as her use of the anaphoric "please." These patterns had
accrued in her work poem by poem. Our previous sessions, and
all the conversations about pattern and language they entailed,
formed a practice that allowed me to "grownd" my listening.
These exchanges are true to Hannah's vision, asking and affirm-
ing, assuring the reader a consensual space where our ways can
cross and knot and kiss. You may occasionally feel turned upside
down when encountering these poems, thrown into a momen-
tary disequilibrium. Motioned truth can throttle even the most
seasoned reader, but the momentary hell of disequilibrium is
sometimes where we must begin. There is great solace in begin-
ning there together, a multiplication of greats that help grownd

us in the simple grace of being gathered, of the possibility of belonging to each other.

Hannah is insistent that we keep each other in the flow and in the light. It was in this context that she revealed the term she uses for poets: "keepers of the light," those committed to cultivate and keep the illuminations we need. In this phrase I hear the echoes of poet-activist Audre Lorde: "Poetry is not a luxury. It is a vital necessity of our existence. It forms the quality of light within which we predicate our hopes and dreams toward survival and change."[13] In and against the consistent imposition of fear and silence, we must seek the illuminative means to see and sing. And it mattered to Lorde that we seek it together, even or especially across difference, without ever minimizing or eliding those differences. Hannah and I couldn't agree more, believing that these lights are nothing if not shared—that the light only exits, in fact, when it leaps forth in the space between us and becomes a bridge we keep together.

Many have noted how this pandemic moment, paced by the Uprising for racial justice, is pushing us to recognize new bridges to new futures, a moment of species-scale struggle through which we might discover the grace of a way forward. We find ourselves in the midst of an unprecedented proliferation of ways of being in the world, spectrums upon spectrums. To paraphrase emergent strategist adrienne maree brown, we can feel ourselves palpably taking part in the expansion of the possible.[14] Various ways of embodying gender or sexuality or race or disability, which have always been here, are now flourishing, as we learn to better discern that variousness and make it legible. We are growing into new possibilities of belonging to ourselves and to each other, possibilities that were barely perceptible mere decades ago, and it is often through writing that we are able to sufficiently illuminate those possibilities.[15]

We no longer have to be one side of a false binary that is primarily judged by how it approximates some specious notion of "normal" (white, able, neurotypical, heterosexual) and is penalized for any way in which it might stray from that norm. When bodies are judged as faulty or aberrant or abhorrent, they tend to lose their humanity in the eyes of the person who is judging, which is often the person with the most inherited power. But now the range of humannesses, a range that in most "developed" societies has been restricted to a dense point for centuries, is experiencing its own big bang, unleashing rich waves of complementary difference that move the possible toward horizons we haven't even glimpsed yet. Neurodiversity is not yet at the center of this conversation, but I believe it will be. I believe the insights of neurodivergent people will occupy a crucial place at the expansion's edge, where humanity might once more immerse itself in more-than-human milieus, finding reciprocity with the highly expressive animal and plant forms all around us.

This book is not about *fixing* people. If anything, it is about how society is utterly and elaborately and strategically broken, and how it imposes that brokenness on us all. At its heart, this book is a living document of people courageously laying bare their brilliant unbrokenness in writing. It is a keeping and sharing of light, of love, like what Erin Manning calls "the spark that shapes an enthusiasm that forever exceeds us."[16]

Hannah is never only Hannah, and a poem is never only a poem. As Adam writes, "The individual is not individual but about the collection in movement of arrangements that are dancing the rally."[17] We are dynamic collections of gesture and desire, gathered together in joy and struggle both. As Mark Eati recently reminded me, "No one is a single self." We are multiple and interconnected in our multiplicity. We live in and through relationship. I am a teacher by the grace of my students, a writer by the grace of my readers. I am a father, husband, brother, friend, son, student, and neurodivergent dancer, all by the grace of the partners who have welcomed my participation. I am also an advocate, activist, and accomplice, desiring a future composed of light and care. Above all, I am a listener who loves language and the people who use it. I am a listener who loves language and is learning to better perceive how it suffuses the more-than-human world. I am grateful for your own listening and learning. And I hope, dear reader, that in kissing you upside down, this book becomes far more than a book for you.

Like Water I Am Eager

What Makes Pooh Say Oooh?—Listening and Absorbing—
Awe Arrives—The Smell of Water—A River System of
Incalculable Beauty—Like Water I Always Move—I Game
the Space—Every Poem Is a House Made for Dancing—
Community on the Page

Midway through spelling out the word "c-o-r-i-a-n-d-e-r," a word no one else in the room is quite sure how to spell, Mark begins hopping up and down a full foot into the air on a yoga ball, clapping and laughing and smiling broadly. His teacher, Katie, a thirty-year public school veteran, is wide-eyed at this turn of events, flabbergasted and deeply pleased. Mark is nineteen years old and he's writing a poem, the second he's ever attempted. The line he's just written seems to flood his body with sensory excitement: "Awe arrives as the taste of coriander spice."

Katie is doubly surprised because, unlike many autistic students who revel in self-stimulatory movements (stims) like flapping or twallowing, Mark is most often engaged by a meditative calm. Seated in his bright patterned shirt, his black hair cascading over his shoulders, he appears to almost hover. His back is aligned into a soft and tensile curve, firm without rigidity.

He is silent, and slightly beaming. But all this seems to change when Mark writes poetry. In the midst of poetry's sensory and intellectual thrall, Mark teems with movement, his placid calm breaking into smile and gesture and exuberant sound.

I entered Katie's classroom at the South Education Center in Richfield, Minnesota, expecting to work with Mark's peer, Shana, who was locally renowned for writing poetry from her own nonspeaking perspective. I'd recently been introduced to a chapbook of her poems at the Autism Society of Minnesota offices. If it weren't for Shana, I might never have met Mark, who on this day was watching a video on his iPad of a parade at Disneyland. He was engrossed by the characters promenading down a street lined with howling fans; the sky occasionally pulsated with fireworks. When the video was over, I suggested we write about it. I quickly added that I didn't want to limit him to Disney material and that I was sure he had plenty of sophisticated ideas to share as well. He looked at me calmly and quizzically, neither impeding nor supporting the idea, as far as I could tell.

I began in a whimsical vein, riffing and rhyming with the characters we'd just seen. I asked, "What makes Mickey feel icky?" Mark thought for a while. His iPad was open in front of him to preprogrammed categories. Katie prompted him with possible choices—a food? a smell? a motion?—and Mark tentatively began to touch icons on the screen, navigating toward an answer: first animals, then insects, then a ladybug. This process took about fifteen minutes. I typed "A ladybug makes Mickey feel icky" on the illuminated and interactive whiteboard at the front of the classroom. Then I asked, "What makes Donald Duck say yuck?" He was slightly quicker this time, again choosing animals before finally settling on a rabbit. Though his answers weren't exactly logical, I appreciated the way they ran poetically askew. As a poet, I am always looking to be surprised, and Mark's choices intrigued me.

Finally I asked, "What makes Pooh say oooh?" Mark looked at me and then at his iPad for several minutes, finger hovering over different categories while Katie and I encouraged him with possible answers. A bell rang, indicating the end of the class period. Mark grew visibly frustrated, his eyes straining wide and his mouth drawing back into a scowl. Part of me felt the need to gather my things and make it to my next class, while another part of me could see that Mark was not done trying. I wanted to respect his efforts, even if I couldn't yet read what they were marshaling toward. The sensorimotor complexity that Mark was endeavoring to navigate was a more intense version of what we all face at particular moments. Who hasn't found themselves stuck in the cross fire of conflicting impulses or speechless in front of an expectant room? While I was still trying to decide whether it was more important for me to be on time for my next student or remain present for Mark, he touched open a keyboard on the screen and quickly, resolutely, typed "AWED."

A complex answer, but Mark typed it simply—as if it were something he did every day. In months of working with him, however, neither Katie nor Mark's educational aide (EA) had ever seen him type a single letter on the keyboard of his iPad, nor activate it independently. They looked at me like I was a magician, maybe even a charlatan. If it hadn't been for their faces, I never would have guessed that something so unimaginable had just transpired. And looking back now, it doesn't surprise me that Winnie the Pooh, the most Buddha-like character in all of children's literature, was the impetus. It also didn't completely surprise me when, a few months later, I sat down with Mark's mother, Indu, and learned that this wasn't the first time Mark had brought his intellect into the light.

. . .

Indu and I met at a restaurant down the street from my house. After some brief small talk, we moved into deeper matters. Looking at me intensely, Indu said, "I have to tell you about the math." She had a look on her face that simultaneously said "Prepare yourself" and "There is nothing that could prepare you for what I'm about to say."

Mark was diagnosed with autism at twenty months of age. A month later, he began intensive applied behavioral analysis (ABA) therapy. The prevailing autism therapy for more than forty years, ABA emphasizes learning through reinforcement. Certain activities are repeated over and over, rewarding correct answers (or behaviors) and negatively reinforcing others. ABA's use of negative reinforcement often elides the line between learning and punishment, but Mark's therapists were relatively gentle in their approach.[1]

After a *full year* of *all-day* ABA therapy, everyone decided it was best to take a week off for spring break. The main goal they'd been doggedly pursuing was, on the surface, outrageously simple: they wanted Mark to distinguish between "cat" and "ball." These words and others were written on torn pieces of paper and placed before him, over and over. The tearing itself was used as an auditory stimulus, designed to draw his attention

to the process, not unlike the way line breaks visually alert read-
ers to the progression of a poem. But things weren't progressing.
Indu *knew* her child was thinking. She *knew* her child possessed
intellect. She recognized, in her child's eyes, an intelligence at
work. An intelligence that went far beyond cat and ball.

The next day Indu placed Mark in a favorite indoor swing.
As with many autists, swinging helped calm and organize
Mark's body and mind. A nursery rhyme was playing on the
stereo, a sort of addition table set to song: *one plus one is two,
two plus two is four, four plus four is eight*, etc. Indu looked at
Mark and saw that his face, his *expression*, had changed. It was
smiling, engaged, processing, acknowledging. And Indu *knew*.
She immediately used the ABA techniques to test whether
Mark understood numbers. She ripped the paper and wrote
six different possible answers to a question: What is one plus
one? After Mark pointed to the right answer from among the
possibilities, Indu started over and asked a more complicated
question: What is two plus three? *Rip*. What is nine plus seven?
Rip. What is five times three? *Rip*. Not only was Mark getting
all the answers correct, but he never required more than a lit-
eral second of thought before reaching out for the correct piece
of paper. By the time Monday arrived, Indu had discovered
that there was virtually no end to his computational abilities.
He could multiply 1,257 times 2,754 before Indu was even
done laying down the choices. And his intellect wasn't lim-
ited to numbers, either. Indu tested Mark for letter, word, and
sentence recognition—*rip rip rip*—only to find that he was
hyperlexical as well. Mark wasn't even three years old yet, and
his internal database of numbers and letters dwarfed that of
children three times his age. *Rip*. Indu did some research and

discovered that Mark was part of a tiny but nonetheless real lineage of computational savants, including his now-famous contemporary Daniel Tammet.[2]

For a few months Mark's ABA therapists were able to keep his interest by engaging in math-related exchanges. Then, just like that, Mark retreated once more. Whether it was the particular ABA interface, the stagnant levels of mathematical complexity, something plainly neurodevelopmental (as if our brains could ever be plain), or some mysterious combination of these factors, by age three he appeared to have settled into a form of deep interiority. Mark was there and not there, socially distant while seemingly ultrapresent in some larger private world Indu could only faintly imagine. This is how he moved through the world for nearly seventeen years. When he typed the word "AWED," Mark signaled his readiness to move in a different way.

· · ·

Now Mark can describe those years himself: "During that time, I was listening and absorbing. I did not willingly express myself until I was shown how to focus and express. Typing skills and feeling listened to helped the most. ABA and other therapies were boring and they did not focus on my strengths. I was subjected to boring classes. I was taken for granted because I could not express myself. I hated being taken for granted. People assumed I did not know anything."

I also *hate* that Mark was taken for granted—no word is strong enough for the breadth of that disregard—and I am grateful for his resilience and grace, his impossible equanimity. Although he was not expressing himself through language, Mark was developing the means to do so, patiently cultivating a voice he could turn to when the moment was right. Just as reading and listening fuel my own writing, Mark was preparing his way toward the poem all along, through an act of sustained and generative receptivity. Mark remembers this time of listening and absorbing as a source of continuous creative development and growth.

For Mark's story to echo through classrooms and group homes and teachers' lounges and domed government buildings, it has to carry all that is simple and complex about him. For instance, it's a simple matter to say he doesn't speak. A more complex (and accurate) appraisal would be that Mark's sensorimotor difficulties almost entirely limit his access to speech. It is simple to say he has uttered no more than a mere and disconnected handful of words in his life. Yet the reasons why those words arose is not a simple matter. In each case, it happened suddenly and without premeditation. Those of us with fluidly functioning throats and tongues and mouths cannot imagine the kind of complex motor organization it takes to produce something as simple as a word, but for many nonspeaking autists a single word can take years of concentrated effort.

Recent studies have shown a significant overlap between autism and other diagnoses, like Parkinson's, that are characterized by foundational motor differences. A wide-ranging look at this phenomenon was published in the compendium *Autism: The Movement Sensing Perspective*, which works to shift the focus from qualitative psychological observation to highly interdisciplinary quantitative assessments. A central question the editors ask is this: "Can high level cognitive processes and behaviors be identified as the core issues people with autism face, or do these characteristics perhaps often rather reflect individual attempts to cope with underlying physiological issues?"[3] The book's research firmly points to the latter possibility, underlining how behavior and cognition might actually be the product of something more foundational. This might seem obvious, and yet autism has consistently been defined in terms of social deficit, rather than as a difference in sensory and movement experience.

In her foreword to the book, Geraldine Dawson writes that the collection catalyzes this shift by positing, "Differences in sensory and motor abilities are primary and social interaction deficits are secondary."[4] In other words, the editors and authors desire a world where, with care, we look at what bodies *do* and *how* they do it before we ever surmise about *what* they think and mean and are. This seemingly small shift in perspective has marked a watershed in thinking *with* autism and autistic individuals. Researchers are beginning to move away from defining what autism *is* and toward what autism might *feel* like.

It's impossible to overstate the negative effects that the overpsychologicalization of autism has had on autistic lives. By enacting a Cartesian divorce of the mind from the body, medical scholarship has historically placed autism within the realm of medicalized psychopathology, often stripping autists of their rights and agency. This imbalanced emphasis on the mind also led to a string of Freudian hypotheses for the cause of autism that have been incredibly destructive to both autists and their families.

For individuals who are struggling mightily with motor difference, any systemic undermining of their ability to be intentional is devastating. As M. Remi Yergeau writes, "Autism is medically construed as a series of involuntarities—of thought, mode, action, and being."[5] Each framing of autism as synonymous with "broken" or "unthinking" or "unwell" increases the harrowing distance between autistic individuals and their rights to self-determination. But we know, now, that there is no mind separate from the body, and new research shows that autists experience a plethora of interwoven sensory and motor phenomena that require incredibly nuanced support and understanding to navigate.

This research is finally allowing scientists to erode the pervasive belief of languagelessness among nonspeaking autists, who themselves obliterate this presumption when given the supports they need to demonstrate an often prodigious capacity for languaging. Researchers like Alexandra Woolgar at Cambridge University are working to develop neuroimaging tests to disprove, once and for all, the damaging presumption of language impairment among nonspeaking autists:

> For decades, science has assumed that nonspeaking autistic people do not speak because they have major language impairments. But in the last few years anecdotal evidence from across the world has been piling up against this assumption—nonspeakers have written books, blogs, poems and more, demonstrating incredible language prowess. The research field has a lot of catching up to do!

In our work, we hope to bypass the requirement for motor responses, and study language comprehension directly by measuring neural responses using brain imaging. We hope to develop a technique that is sensitive enough to track understanding in individual children, and use it to find out how commonly nonspeakers have good language skills—especially those that do not yet have an alternative form of communication. We hope that this will contribute to turning the tide on how scientists, clinicians, carers and families think about, and treat, people who do not speak.[6]

It's hard to overstate the importance we place in our society on the performance of language. There is often a strict equivalence between speech (a particular kind of speech privileged by the dominant culture) and value. Because Mark did not speak, sign, or type when I first met him, most people assumed that he was without intellect—an assumption that had been consistent for the previous seventeen years of his life. But his family and his teachers at the South Education Center knew better. In our first hour together, he managed a single autonomous typed word, a monosyllabic word that was, ostensibly, a miracle. And despite my sustained awe at the continuous unfolding of his lyrical expression, there is nothing miraculous about his capacity or desire for it. Like everyone else, Mark wanted to find his own song and see how it might contribute to a larger harmony. Wanting to sing ourselves into this world is a foundational part of being human. And so is our collective desire to rewrite our shared world in choral form. Only together can we register the full breadth of awe that our braided existence entails.

· · ·

When I next visit Mark's class at SEC, I have been thinking about "awed" for the entire week, grateful for that word and the world it might open up moving forward. I tell this to Mark and ask if he wants to write a poem about awe that is grounded in the five senses. This time he smiles excitedly, indicating his willingness. But it soon becomes clear that his willingness doesn't automatically will his body into seamless sensorimotor action. As is often the case for nonspeaking autists, Mark's development as a communicator is not destined to be linear. Because he can't immediately summon the ability to type again, we will seek out ways to meet him where he is today, using accommodations to bridge the gap between there and where he wants to go. Because autism is characterized by a desire for repetition and its grounding force, the first accommodation I offer is to begin each line in an identical and predictable fashion. In the medical community this is called "perseveration." Among poets this is called "anaphora." Perseveration is generally considered a deficit, a flaw that bespeaks faulty wiring. In poetry circles, where intellect is generally presumed, it is considered an intentional and fundamental tool.

I ask Mark to choose between three possible verbs: awe *comes*, awe *is*, or awe *arrives*. Although his EA doesn't realize we are echoing Mark's experience with ABA, he writes these three possibilities on a piece of paper. Luckily, Mark seems unfazed by this coincidence and is able to choose "arrives." The first line begins, "Awe arrives as." We will have not only anaphora, but alliteration as well. I ask him to choose a sound. Using the categories on his iPad he first indicates musical instruments and then, more specifically, string instruments, represented by an image of violins. I ask whether Mark prefers "violins" or "string instruments." Again, he pursues the alliterative through-line. We're off to a good start: "Awe arrives as the sound of string instruments."

To set the table for Mark's second line I write, "Awe arrives as the feel of . . ." Mark stares at his iPad, but doesn't touch it. Thinking hard, he looks up at us a couple of times with a quizzical expression. While Katie and Mark's EA prompt him, I watch Mark's fingers. They are methodically making small circles on the surface of his shirt. There is more than one way to communicate. While others might consider it too mundane for a poem about awe, I ask Mark if he is trying to indicate his shirt. His aide writes "yes" or "no," and he chooses "yes." Katie observes that Mark takes great pleasure in wearing brightly patterned shirts with toothsome textures. Wanting to follow the alliterative patterns he's established, I ask Mark if he likes to touch the shirt because it's soft, silky, or smooth. His EA again writes these words down, and he chooses "silky," extending the *L* sound from "feel." The second line of his poem becomes, "Awe arrives as the feel of a silky shirt."

For the third line, we try something a little different. For the past few months, Mark has also been learning something called the rapid prompting method (RPM), which was developed out of necessity and resourcefulness by Soma Mukhopadhyay as a way of helping her son, Tito, a nonspeaking autist, access linguistic expression. Tito and Soma emigrated from India to the United States and now live in Austin, Texas, where Soma teaches the fundamentals of RPM and Tito is a world-renowned poet and memoirist.

RPM involves progressing from three vertically held letter boards with large cutout letters to a single laminated letter board with smaller letters to a similar letter board set flat on a table to approximate a keyboard. After that, the student moves to an actual computer keyboard. At first the student is asked to hold a pencil and poke it through letter shapes that are cut out of the board, indicating words one letter at a time. Though the process is laborious, it also engages the student's sensory apparatus, hoping to marshal the pleasure of sensory engagement toward expression. Mark has been practicing, but he is still very much at the beginning of the RPM learning curve and has shown limited stamina for spelling in this manner.

While I write "Awe arrives as the taste of . . ." on the interactive whiteboard, Mark's EA pulls out his letter boards and I ask Mark what taste creates a sense of awe for him. Upon hearing the word "taste," he becomes happily frenetic, smiling and bouncing on his yoga ball. This minor stimming behavior makes it even harder for him to successfully spell out an answer, but he seems intent. Because Katie knows how much Mark loves his grandmother's Indian cooking, she prompts him with different dishes and spices. Slowly, but resolutely, he indicates five letters, one at a time, spelling out the word "spice." I ask whether he'd like to see (or taste) a particular spice in this line, and his smile widens, his stimming brimming further. As Katie and I begin discussing different Indian spices, Mark is nearly bursting with a never-before-seen eagerness to use his letter boards. Quickly and correctly, with astounding fine motor accuracy, he spells out "coriander," and the moment his finger pokes through the final cutout letter *R*, he begins jumping into the air and clapping the insides of his wrists together, beaming a gorgeous full-toothed smile, as if he's just pitched the final out in game seven of the World Series. Pride fills the room like some kind of coriander-scented helium. We're all giddy with it. "Awe arrives as the taste of coriander spice."

Like "awed" at the close of our first session, "coriander" simultaneously charged and grounded Mark's ability to language himself for others. In the context of a poem, with its distinctively patterned approach to language, these words functioned as access points, engaging his intellect and facilitating his expression. I have found that each student has their own set of access points, words that possess an almost talismanic power. They carry a certain gravity that allows other words to constellate, orienting expression. Their magnetism allows the body itself to constellate its movements into legibility and illumination. This is the magic spell inherent to spelling, the wonder of putting these little marks on the page or screen. If you can find the marks that suit the moment (or the Mark), the letters that let light in, then merely by appearing they can open up unforeseen universes of possibility and connection.

And the poem isn't even complete! In the fourth line, Mark invites an unlikely animal into the poem: "Awe arrives as the sight of a seal." Continuing the alliterations found earlier with "sound of string" and "silky shirt," Mark chooses to alliterate "sight" and "seal," letting the sibilant sonic elements emphasize the seen. I love how this unexpected choice highlights the corporeal strangeness of the seal's sleek yet amorphous body. This is one of my favorite moments as a teacher who is always also a poet—when a student reorients my relationship to language through a surprising simile.

In the final line of the poem, Mark transforms this abstract exercise in sensory experience into something refreshingly hands-on. Following the beginning of the line "Awe arrives as the smell of . . . ," he quickly pushes his iPad's water icon. His EA brings him a drink, and Katie comments on Mark's love of water. When he's finished the entire glass, I ask again about our final line. He touches the water icon once more, a voice from the iPad intoning *water*. His EA says Mark would drink water all day if he could. While this observation is surely born of experience, it strikes me as a brush-off of sorts. These kinds of seemingly minor dismissals can cause an autist, struggling to be heard, anguish. On the other hand, if a teacher remains open to the various forms communication might take, and actively curious in their listening, then the student has more opportunities to make themselves heard and known. Again, sometimes doing nothing but listening intently, holding a space for the student, can be the most helpful role a teacher can take.

After a moment, I wonder aloud whether water is exactly what Mark intends here. I tentatively complete the line so Mark can see it, "Awe arrives as the smell of water," and he looks pleased, his hand retreating from the iPad. I ask whether the line is the way he wants it, and Mark uses the letter board to answer Y-E-S. Like many autists, his sensory experience of the world is incredibly rich and layered, almost incomprehensibly refined. Mark *smells* water. And though that might seem completely normal to him, water remains monolithically neutral to most people, something that appeals to the senses only in moments of urgent, desert-induced thirst. Mark smells water the way I smell coffee. Water, that most humble form of sustenance, brings him awe:

Awed

Awe arrives as the sound of string instruments
Awe arrives as the feel of a silky shirt
Awe arrives as the taste of coriander spice
Awe arrives as the sight of a seal
Awe arrives as the smell of water

Katie steeps in the awe of one whose well-hewn instinct about and belief in a student has, against all odds, been affirmed. I feel waves of awe, too, finding myself a witness to this classroom's transformation, watching vectors of joy carom between our four faces. I learn once more how much poetry can alter the world.

In going from the bright taste of coriander to the exquisitely refined smell of water, Mark demonstrated the sensory acuity I would come to expect from him in the coming months. Years later, when I asked him about this moment, he typed: "Operating in poetic expression is very pleasing to my senses. I could not only sense the smell of coriander, but I could taste and feel it in my body. It was like thunder and lightning striking a tree. It was an amazing feeling. Poetic messages can have a deeper impact on my brain compared to other messages that can be ignored."

. . .

These poetic messages, replete with formalized repetition and rooted in sensory detail, offered Mark the linguistic possibility he was seeking. The language practices that had surrounded him weren't able to carry the language he had in his mind. For Mark this was the beginning of a sustained exploration into what his language practices were and how poetry, among other forms, could meet those practices wherever he was—as a writer, an autist, an activist, a human being, and all at once.

In *Autistic Disturbances: Theorizing Autism Poetics from the* DSM *to* Robinson Crusoe, Julia Miele Rodas outlines the possible existence of an autistic dialect: "A survey of literature on autistic language—including writing by clinicians, by literary scholars, and by autists, sometimes in overlapping roles—does indicate, contrary to popular notions, that autism may be said to have its own language, its own distinctive forms of verbal expression."[7] And lest we fall into the trap of conscribing autism into yet another oppressive and limited frame, Rodas helpfully reminds us: "Pointing to the existence of an autistic expressive fingerprint . . . must not be construed as constraint, a roping off of autistic expressive idiosyncrasies into some restricted ward or ghetto."[8]

After working with autistic poets, both speaking and non-speaking, for more than fifteen years, I've been delighted to recognize how many of them possess their own highly specific idiolects, recognizable by unique and often surprising linguistic patterns.[9] And furthermore, it's been an equal delight to recognize how those patterns resonate with and diverge from their peers. As Adam and Estée are forever reminding me: diversity in neurodiversity. The autistic tongue might be seen as a river system of incalculable beauty and complexity, rife with headwaters, tributaries, streams, and even momentary eddies. The languagings present in that system are staggering, both in their specificity and in the ways those various specificities—"unexpected, outspoken, rich, florid"[10]—tap (and feed) shared reservoirs of poetic and conceptual resources. And this fluidity helps complicate and elaborate the solidarities these languagings engender. As Angela Davis says, "Our solidarities will be complex."[11]

When I first meet a student, acknowledging the patterns that constitute their particular languaging is among my most vital priorities, and that acknowledgment requires many weeks of deep listening. It's crucial that I don't alienate the emergence of those patterns by attempting in any way to correct or normalize them. As with any student I work with, no matter their neurotype or poetic experience, I'm looking to reflect back the language practices that seem most true to what the student is trying to do and say. But it's like I'm learning a language for the first time, so I have to try to leave all my preconceptions behind. As with any relationship, the student needs to get to know me as much as I need to get to know them. Which means I have to build trust and foster ease, which is easier said than done. With some students, that trust comes quickly; with others, it is more gradual. I've come to think of my role as grounded in a practice of kind, open, receptive, and close reading. While this makes me grateful for my English degree, I also know it means I have to actively eschew traditional modes of reading and knowing. Because my students are so often autodidacts, their engagement with language is incredibly specific. I want to nurture that specificity with as much generosity and space as I can muster. Furthermore, I have to stay vigilant, because these remarkable ways of languaging, like any living language, change as they deepen and develop over time.

Identifying subject matter that suits a neurodivergent student is often self-evident, in large part because of what the medical literature calls a "restricted interest," a term used to describe the autistic tendency to pursue topics with "abnormal intensity or focus." Since I have pursued poetry and poetic forms with an abnormal intensity and focus for many years, it wasn't hard for me to see how this shared trait was also a tremendous gift. In the realm of the poetic, "restricted interests," and their concomitant perseverative impulses, are far from deficits; they are the key to connecting with neurodivergent learners and giving them the tools to connect with others. The author Dara McAnulty says it perfectly:

> When we (by "we" I mean autistics) get interested in something, most people would call it an "obsession." It really is not an obsession, though. It's not dangerous, quite the opposite. It's liberating and essential to the workings of my brain. It calms and soothes: gathering information, finding patterns, sequencing and sorting out is a muscle I must flex. I prefer the word passion. Yes! And it's absolutely essential that we get to follow our passions.[12]

Among my nonspeaking students, I find that language is itself often a passion that exceeds the others.[13] Each student wields a different set of linguistic and lyrical patterns to achieve their voice, and yet each of these voices exhibits a similar penchant for sensory-rich, embodied, and impassioned writing.[14] For many of my nonspeaking students, this poetic voice is virtually synonymous with their intrinsic voice. In other words, the linguistic patterns they use to communicate outside of poetic writing are the same linguistic patterns they use to communicate within their poems. Whereas my "poetic voice" is much different from the one I use to construct this sentence, their voices remain consistent across genre or context. In my experience, the dynamic structure and nonnormative forms of poetry provide the most varied palette of opportunities for nonspeaking students to bring the full force and authenticity of their voices into expression.

Adam Wolfond, the nonspeaking poet and artist you met in the Introduction, wields a gloriously idiosyncratic language (or *parole* as he sometimes puns in French). In the years since I began working with Adam, I have looked forward to each one-hour session as another opportunity to delve further into the patterned complexity of his voice, which reels with and revels in the dynamic movement of natural forms.

. . .

Adam's smile has stamina and wattage. It's rarely missing, even when he is thinking through a received hurt or some furtive grief. He brims and he stims and sometimes he overspills, jumping off the couch to find a rubber bath toy or a half-peeled stick, something that comforts him with its texture and sound. Though a thousand miles usually separate us, I know in great detail the variety of sounds he makes, often finding their crescendo in an eager, open-throated, baritone vowel that he holds for several seconds.[15]

For Adam, the most difficult aspect of writing is falling into the concentrated physical stillness necessary to type. Movement—propulsive, fidgety, sometimes racing—is the way Adam routinely greets the world. And since he repeatedly writes about thinking with his body, this movement is characteristic of his bracingly vibrant mind. His mother, Estée, a prodigious artist and thinker herself, calmly beckons Adam toward a momentary typing harbor. After sweeping around the room like a handsome typhoon, he finally makes landfall amid a lumpy helping of pillows, and Estée places a hand upon his shoulder, smoothing out Adam's boisterous nervous system. Soon he is ready to direct his generous energy toward language. A thousand miles away, connected by my desktop screen, I excitedly ready myself for the ride.

I am less Adam's teacher and more his amanuensis, hurriedly following the poetic shapes of gushing lyric that fluidly pour forth from his single typing finger. As he wrote when I was first getting to know him: "Like water I am eager / Like water I am thinking / Like water I always move." These lines are characteristic of Adam's writing, which often emerges in patterns of three. Since water is a constituent part of Adam's being in the world, I call it his three-wave pattern, like the grouped set of waves for which a surfer eagerly watches.

As you read this poem, allow your body to feel each curve and carve and swell:

The Maker of Wanting Space

I want to say that I want
to amazing space think
about the way I move
to think

I game the space the way
I open with the body and the way
I think which is the way
of water

It touches me open and I am
away with really easy feelings
of dancing for the answering
really rare always rallying
thinking and it is rare with the way
people think

Really way of touching the world is
the way I am wanting with
my tics

I think that I want the way inside
questions opening the want to
the wanting way which thinks openly
toward the water and I am
thinking about it all
the time

I think that I want the way inside
questions opening the want to
the wanting way which thinks openly
toward the water and I am
thinking about it all the time like
eating words

When I reread that first stanza, I hear how the waves break where the lines do, emphasizing certain ideas that help bring the content into focus. When Adam writes "I want to say that I want," he is underscoring the eagerness that characterizes his way of being in the world—the wanting force of desire that repeats and overspills, leading us "to amazing space think" our way into more capacious architectures. These are spaces in which Adam can move unobstructed by the narrow measures of grammar and embark on a journey of free and thoughtful choreography where each gesture details "the way I move / to think." Here the third wave finally breaks upon the shore of thought, axiomatically linking movement with meaning, process with product. In three waves, Adam has initiated the reader into his poetics of desire, expression, dance, space, and metacognition. Adam's perspective on the world is not insular but seeks always to connect with others and to help them see the world anew.

Adam turns "the way" into a guidepost for the reader, establishing a pattern of breaks that usher us through the turns. As he works to "game the space," he returns over and over to that bright *A* sound—game, space, way—cracking open the music of the poem. This gaming of space gets right to the heart of poetic writing, which always seeks new ways to leverage the patterns of language against the frame of the page. In poetry each section of empty space plays its own role, forging contrast until it nearly glows: a potential-laden latency posing as silence. Adam employs a poetic fluidity, allowing him to touch everything without obscuring anything.

Although his language is surprising and idiosyncratic, Adam seeks clarity. He endows his work with the potential for self-advocacy and revelation. Over the years, Adam has encountered countless questions about autism, many of them dry and predictable. Neurotypical interrogators often want to skip over the nuance of autistic embodiment and just have things explained, but Adam wants more. His first chapbook was titled *In Way of Music Water Answers Towards Questions Other Than What Is Autism.* Poetry gives Adam a space where he has the opportunity to be most himself, a young man who seeks the tactile adventure of open forms. And he wants, above all, for others to join him in this adventure. One of his poems ends with the statement: "I think people / don't take the time / to explore / their steps and that / means they just think / about their own without / extending / the choreography."

. . .

This eagerness for dynamic forms and open spaces, Adam's "dancing for the answering," makes him a natural poet. Or, conversely, you could say poetry's ability to nurture what Adam calls "really rare always rallying thinking" makes it a perfect fit for him. Both are true, of course, and this reciprocity between poetry and autism is often entwined with poetry's structural possibilities, which provide a generative space for neurodivergent writers.

As I'm fond of telling my students, *Every poem is a house made for dancing.* At the etymological root of "poetry" sits the Greek *poiesis*: to make or build or compose. In the writing of a poem you are building something with dimensions. And you are building it with intention. There are countless ways to build it and countless building materials to use—that's one of the things

I find so compelling about poetry as a linguistic art form—but it helps to think of the largest building block as the stanza. When I first learned that *stanza* was Italian for "room," everything I'd been doing intuitively as a poet, all that dimensional intentionality, suddenly coalesced into a comprehensible framework. Of course! The poem is a house! And this is one reason why I think so much about—why I dwell on—the hospitality we use to invite others into the practice of reading and writing poems.

And like any good host, I tend to dwell on the kinds of things that happen in the rooms of the house we call a poem. I pace and circulate the rooms, dwelling on the differences between poetry and prose, and eventually I stumble upon verse. It's no coincidence that verse is synonymous with song, but its etymological root turns out to be far more agricultural. While the Latin *versus* might seem to evidence an opposition, it more directly relates to the act of turning. Specifically, it indicates the kind of turn one makes at the end of a row while plowing or planting. And it can also mean to turn an exhausted field over, to let it lie fallow awhile before returning to it with new seed. These are all nutritive metaphors for the act of breaking lines in poetry, turning and returning. A poem is something built out of rooms occupied by the practice of turning. And since the turning of a poem is accomplished on foot—spondee, iamb, dactyl—what else would we call it but dancing?

When you finally enter the house made for dancing, you might draw a few initial conclusions. For one, a poem, which is too often seen as flatly two-dimensional and leashed to the left margin, has the power to leap or roll or stim off and across the page. Another conclusion—and this is something I can't emphasize enough—is that poetry isn't something one does alone.

A poem, in its generous space and playful approach, is an invitation to dance—with other poems, other poets, voices long since disappeared from the aural realm. You may even be dancing with other versions of yourself, the full chorus line of self that crowds and complicates our ability to form a cohesive and individual mode of being. Even if you extend your hand only to the anonymous future reader, and even if that reader is first and foremost yourself, the poem you've built to share with them is an act of radical hospitality, making space for unexpected collaborations and choreographies.

Adam writes that "touching the world is / the way I am wanting with / my tics." Certain movements and sounds that seem out of the ordinary to others form the basic engagement between Adam and the world around him. They are a type of echolocation allowing him to orient his body in space, to find his way in and through the world. Many autists have difficulty with proprioception, the ability to locate one's body within the shifting spaces of the often-overwhelming sensory environment. Every room—with its complex constellation of colorful objects and echoing sounds and alluring smells and moving bodies—can seem like a busy Brooklyn intersection during lunch rush. Stimming movements, like the way Adam twallows a cleanly stripped branch between his fingers or how Mark softly grazes the back of his hand against his cheek, can center an autistic body in both senses of the word: inviting calm while also locating the body in space. The same can be true of sounds: quick, high-pitched yelps created at the roof of the mouth or more resonant, drawn-out tones produced in the throat. As Adam writes, "I am . . . the assembly of talking tics / and I am the masterful ticcer." But despite Adam's mastery, these movements and sounds do not appear ordinary to most people, many of whom have been conditioned by a neuronormative culture to fear the extraordinary. Some of those people bear prejudices that even Adam's hospitable smile can't defuse.

Just a few weeks before I wrote this, Adam was harassed in the street by a concierge who felt threatened by Adam's particular choreography. She barked at him and his support assistant, telling them he "shouldn't be taken out." The ignorance and ableism Adam faces daily are staggering. And so is his resilience. "The law always wants us to be the same," he wrote on his Facebook page. "It sucks to go to the outside world and have to control the body but amazing thought is the questioning of the law. I would like to question the way the law wants all bodies to be the same. I think that the system wants us all to be the same because lots of people are afraid of diversity."

There is ableist thought and there is "amazing thought," a disruption or circumvention or elaboration of the so-called ordinary. One enforces a punitive system riddled with homogenized ideas, and the other engages an open future where difference moves the dance forward. Adam and other nonspeaking autists, refusing to be silenced by those who fear difference, are providing the guideposts to a neurodiverse future. If we can begin to incorporate different modes of movement, of communication, of being and signing and pointing and singing and ticcing and typing, we can foster a collective and mindful mastery of what it means to be human.

Until then, Mark and Adam will continue to write poems, each one a collection of rooms that together form a house, and these poems will begin the hard work of envisioning a future where poetic houses can gather, forming a neighborhood of sorts. Poems are a place where we set about the ethical labor of exploring how we occupy space. The ways we move in and through poems can signal possibilities for how we might move in and through the world. Having written their way into community on the page, Mark and Adam are searching for ways to build community off of it. Adam, with the help of family and friends, co-created The A Collective, which has become *dis assembly*, an emergent group of neurodiverse artists and educators who want to investigate how creativity and community intersect. Mark has teamed up with Max and Indu to form the Autism Sibs Universe (ASU), a nonprofit whose goal is to establish the first neurodiversity-focused cohousing community in Minnesota. These talented autists, building and dancing one interdependent letter at a time, are finding ways to inhabit a world where amazing thought lays the groundwork for inclusive futures.

A Place Where the Islands Touch

The Sharp Call—What Scares Us About Poetry?—
Languaging My Way—Empathy Toward the Trapped
Air—An Area of Devoted Study—Interdependence—
Boxes in Boxes in Boxes—A Linguistic Headwater—
Cryptozoological Cousins—A Spectrum Kids' Guide to
A Wrinkle in Time

Ryan tracked me down in the hallway where I was pushing a
rusty cart overflowing with books from classroom to class-
room. Since hiring me the previous fall, he'd already asked me
to create a mobile library, start a rap composition club, and teach
comic book design. Last week I'd become the middle school
girls' basketball coach. The after-school program was situated
in a sprawling public school at the border of two largely un-
gentrified south Brooklyn neighborhoods and featured an arts-
focused curriculum.

"When you're done making the rounds, head back to 402.
I want you to work with Matteo." I'd seen Matteo eating
Cheez-Its in the cafeteria, but we hadn't been acquainted. Ryan,
the program director, said the other teaching-artists were strug-
gling to integrate him into their activities. He'd heard from

Matteo's daytime teachers as well, and they were completely flummoxed at how to get him involved.

"The thing is," Ryan said with one eyebrow raised, "he talks about only one thing." He paused for effect.

"Well, what is it?" I asked. His apprehension tipped into a slight but guarded look of delight.

"*Planet of the Apes.*"

. . .

I can't tell you how many times I've been having a perfectly cordial conversation with someone—another parent at a kindergarten coffee hour or my dental hygienist—only to have it derail when someone asks me what I do. The moment *poet* makes its tiny plosive arrival, excitedly riding a warm puff of breath from between my lips, things suddenly grow distant and a little cold. It's as if we're suddenly on two different planets, the illusion of our proximity borne away by those two innocuous syllables. Or if not two planets, at least two islands, separated by hundreds of miles of uncrossable ocean.

But it doesn't have to be that way. About ten years ago, I stopped into a local Iowa City gas station to get an oil change, book in hand. When it was done, the mechanic cocked his head to glance at the cover of my book and asked what I was doing in town. I said, a little sheepishly, that I'd moved to town to study poetry. I braced. He looked at me like I was a totally reasonable person and in a mild, even voice said, "Cool." No questions about how I support myself, no blue limericks, just a matter-of-fact acknowledgment from a local mechanic. When the average person finds out I'm a poet, they either gaze at me blankly, like what I've said doesn't compute, or they shoot me a look that's half astonishment and half pity. Then they say, "I could never do that." When I tell them that I work with autistic kids and adults, I encounter the same thing. They say I'm doing "God's work" and I should be very proud of myself and they simply can't imagine how hard it must be.

These kinds of comments lay bare many of the dangerous presumptions that characterize an ableist viewpoint, which imagines what I do as charity and who I serve as a burden. I do this work because I organically discovered that I love doing it. It's a job that brings me pleasure, kinship, and an evergreen source of creative insight that enriches my work as a poet. I am no saint and neither are my students; we are not selfless but, rather, sensitive, and the burdens of the daily world often fall away when we get together. I can't imagine my life without autistic and disabled folk, and I honestly pity anyone who has been conditioned to avoid their company.

Today autism and poetry are outliers, but that hasn't always been the case. Despite the recent "surge" in diagnoses of autism, which is most likely just a reflection of our greater awareness, it isn't a new phenomenon. And if we think beyond (or before) the medical definition of autism, then it's not difficult to see how autistic modes of embodiment and perception have long preceded the categories we use to describe them. I'm far from alone in believing that both poetry and autism have been fundamentally present in human culture since the beginning of human culture, or even before.[1] The practice of language is often used to draw an artificial line between the human and animal, but I see it as a practice that actually connects us to our animate counterparts, animal and otherwise. Autistic writers have helped me see how the entire aural field teems with language, beginning with the leaves and birds.

The experience of synesthesia occurs when two different sensory inputs overlap. For instance, some people see a particular color upon hearing a particular musical note: a teal B-sharp. It's a complex experience that is relatively rare, experienced by roughly 4 percent of the general population. But autists experience synesthesia at more than four times that rate, and experience teaches me that nonspeaking autistic folk experience synesthesia at a rate that is far, far higher.[2] Neurologically speaking, this is not a new phenomenon, so let's picture a young woman at the mouth of a cave. She perceives the *sharp* call of a red-tailed hawk. This sensorial conflation might be a natural gateway for metaphorical thought, bringing one sensation—the sharpness of touch—into alignment with another—the sound of the hawk—allowing the young woman to experience both at the same time. This kind of perceptual interweaving is at the heart of metaphor, expressing how something can be both itself (a sound) and something else (a touch). The expression of this doubleness, this deepening into the multiplicity of experience, might well have formed the soil from which poetry sprang.[3] Our engagements with the more-than-human world of sound and sight (and taste and smell and touch) give rise to poetic experiences that help us, as Pierre Teilhard de Chardin once put it, "sing the universe back to itself."[4]

This is how I understand poetry and autism to be grounded in human (and more-than-human) experience, but today these concepts are often fraught with unhelpful cultural stereotypes that leave them rife with myth and misconception. Poetry is typically seen as an art form best practiced in kindergarten classrooms and ivory towers, but nowhere in between. Autism is popularly embodied by the savant, a brilliant but socially feeble stereotype that either revolutionizes the tech industry or lives in an institution. These characterizations are not only incorrect; they do real damage to individual people and our collective well-being. By relegating autism and poetry to the margins of human experience, we undermine the crucial uses of poetry and the basic humanity of autistic individuals. We often marginalize what we fear. What scares us about poetry? About autism?

One possible answer might be: connection. At their best, poems share something very real about the writer that connects to something very real in the reader. When we read a great poem we think, ah, that's it—a texture, an emotion, an image—I *feel* that. An authentic connection. Which is what I feel in my relationships with autistic folk. I trust my autistic friends to both acknowledge what I feel and grow my understanding of what's possible to feel, allowing me to be more accountable to myself and my community. It's a vulnerable proposition. And one of the reasons autists routinely eschew small talk is that it *feels* insincere, which it often is. Neurotypical culture is rife with insincerities that keep connection at a surface level so it can be easily negotiated, categorized, and moved through with capitalist efficiency.

And this brings me to another possible answer, or maybe even another layer to the answer of connection: pace. This is a concept that Adam Wolfond has made especially legible for me in his writing. To preview a poem that we'll explore in more depth later, Adam writes: "I am / languaging my way the long

/ poetic feelings packing to- / gether the pace of the world." Though poems may be short, poetic feelings are often long and actively language their way at whatever pace they need in order to gather us into their world. And thus "gethered" in a shared ether, we can make space for deeper connections.

The pace of the neurotypical world, on the other hand, is the pace of ableism, capitalism, and neuronormativity. To participate in it, which is tantamount to having value within it, we must move and communicate at a uniform speed. But poems and neurodivergent ways of moving through the world similarly resist this passive capitulation. They offer another way, a proliferation of other ways, articulating various possibilities of pace that dance in response to the more-than-human world—an act that signals nothing less than a rupture with capitalist production. As Erin Manning writes: "Altering the speed at which the everyday tends to function creates openings for neurodiverse forms of perception. It also makes time for modes of encounters otherwise elided."[5]

Sometimes these encounters feel so oddly real that other people instinctively belittle them, looking to escape the radical implications and opportunities they alight. My experience among autists has taught me to welcome this kind of connection, this kind of pace, and to embrace its liberatory potential in the way I embrace the liberatory potential of each poem. In the neurodiverse future I aim myself toward, transactional exchanges between human beings will be supplanted by meaningful encounters, fed by deep currents of respect and curiosity. Perhaps we might approach every person the way we approach a great poem, assuming intellect and intentionality, knowing that our mutual humanity precedes us into every room we enter.

• • •

Within moments of Matteo stepping into the classroom, his dark hair tousled atop black prescription glasses, he confirmed the rumors of his love for the original 1968 *Planet of the Apes* film. The new Tim Burton remake was just released on DVD, but Matteo categorically dismissed it like a gourmand offered a Twinkie. For what it's worth, I agreed. I asked him if he'd like to write some poems with me. He felt neutral about the prospect, which was fair. I tried haiku, a sonnet, some other traditional forms, but none of them seemed attuned to Matteo's exuberance for the film. Finally, with our time wearing thin, I suggested that he simply tell me the film, in his own words, while I dictated. And off we went, creating a novelization of the film in poetic form.

Matteo, often the tersest of pre-teens, was now speaking the film at a pace my hand could hardly match. I found I could moderate his speed by asking questions to draw out greater specificity. Even so, each minute that passed contained more of Matteo's words than he normally spoke in an hour. Nearly every new thought began with "Then," a sort of propulsive adverb that gave his resulting poem centrifugal force as it rounded through the story, like a father's hand speeding a crowded tire swing at each revolution.

When the bell rang, Matteo's eyes widened and he took a settling breath before asking if we could finish the poem tomorrow. I said I'd talk with Ryan to see whether we could work together every day during this period. Matteo nodded and slowly made his way to the door, a soft focus blanketing his eyes. This is a look I would come to recognize over the years, as several other cinephile students described inwardly watching their favorite movies, recollected at will. Often, if I knew them well enough, I could actually guess what was screening inside the theater of their mind. Sometimes even a particular scene. For students like Matteo, this ability to access one's treasured visuals can act as a sort of gel the world needs to pass through if it wants to be seen, making it crucial to begin always with their particular passion.

The next day Matteo began talking before I was able to unclip my pen from my pocket. He saw where we'd left off and launched forward, interrupted only by my questions and clarifications. This was 2003, and I didn't know anything about autism beyond the movie *Rain Man*. Looking back from nearly twenty years into the future, I can see how my ignorance was actually a crucial asset. The prevailing professional framework of the time, solidified in the research of Simon Baron-Cohen, was that autists definitively lacked "theory of mind," or the ability to imagine/anticipate the thoughts/thinking of another person. In the late 1990s, Baron-Cohen developed a diagnostic tool called the Empathy Quotient, which purportedly tested the ability of someone to identify with the feelings of someone else. This and other research fed the troubling idea that autistic people possessed little if any capacity for empathy, a dangerous misconception that often cultivated the mistreatment of autists on the grounds that they were subhuman or unfeeling. We now know that empathy is far more complex than Baron-Cohen understood. In fact, new research is pointing to a "double empathy problem," elucidating how researchers like Baron-Cohen demonstrate exactly the kind of "mindblindness" in relation to autistic people that they see as an essentially autistic trait.[6] If I had been indoctrinated by this research in 2003, I wouldn't have periodically stopped Matteo to inquire about the emotional lives

of the characters or their inner psychology. If I'd been suffi-
ciently conditioned by the era, I may have never engaged him in
the writing of a poem in the first place.

I can't tell you how grateful I am that I didn't know any
better, that I was able to listen beyond the professional precon-
ceptions of the moment. At one point in the poem, Matteo ze-
roed in on the fear felt by primitive humans on the edge of the
forbidden zone. Taylor and his shipmates Landon and Dodge
(Stewart didn't survive the journey) have just stepped into a
waterfall to bathe themselves.

Not only does Matteo name the fear these humans feel in
the poem, a fear he could only know from having read nonver-
bal signs, but he elucidates this fear with the gorgeous meta-
phor of deer fleeing into the foliage, utilizing an internal rhyme
(fear/deer) in the process. I didn't know any better then, but
I do now. A 2009 article by Scottish researcher Adam Smith
found that autistic individuals don't just experience empathy
on levels equal to their neurotypical peers, but in many cases
exceed them. Often autists are wracked by *an excess* of empa-
thy, leading to a systemic form of emotional paralysis.[7] Smith
was able to show that there are actually three successive stages
to what we commonly recognize as empathy—emotional em-
pathy, cognitive empathy, and performative empathy.

Ralph James Savarese, building on Smith's research, writes
about the ways autistic thinkers often find themselves im-
mersed in this first stage, overwhelmed by a flood of emotional
empathy for humans and animals and objects alike, short-
circuiting their ability to name the feeling of empathy for
themselves and then communicate it to others. In an interview
with Tito Mukhopadhyay, Savarese delved into a news story

about a group of trapped Chilean miners. When he invited Tito to share his empathetic experience of the story, he replied:

> My empathy would probably be towards the flashlight bat-teries of those trapped coal miners if there happens to be a selection on my part. Or my empathy would be towards the trapped air around those coal miners. There would be me watching through the eyes of the flashlight cell the utter hopelessness of those unfortunate miners as my last chemicals struggled to glow the faint bulb so that I didn't leave them dying in darkness. As the air around them, I would try to find a way to let myself squeeze every bit of oxygen I have to allow the doomed lungs to breathe, for I am responsible for their doom.[8]

This circuit of empathy, moving by way of relation from miner to flashlight to battery to chemical to air and finally back to miner, balloons a single moment of crisis into a crescendo of interconnected crises.

Repeated viewings of *Planet of the Apes* allowed Matteo to research—by way of dialogue, affect, facial expression—the cri-sis of a main character and how that crisis played out across a spiraling set of ape/man relations. In diagnostic terms, his deep passion for this film would be termed Matteo's restricted inter-est, but I would argue that this interest is restricted only by the ability of others to make connections with it. Matteo's affinity for *Planet of the Apes* constitutes an area of devoted study, and it is our responsibility to learn from this research, both what it says about the film and what it says about Matteo. And what it says about us. Only then can this "restricted" interest transform into the pathway that leads to everywhere and everyone else. It is, in fact, Matteo's key to a life of connection and participation—with all those ready to listen.

. . .

The more I've worked at the intersection of poetry and autism, the more I've come to apprehend the twinlike nature that these two—realms, practices, communities—possess. And it has become clear to me that the parallel margins they inhabit in today's society are falsely constructed. While poets are often figured as heart-stricken loners scribbling in a damp garret by moonlight, the reality is that poetry continues to thrive because it is deeply rooted in the interconnected social fabric of readings, slams, podcasts, and small press culture. Autists, in a similar but far more problematic fashion, have been mischaracterized by a solitary and unreachable interiority. And yet, autistic lives are profoundly interconnected, routinely necessitating the participation of others to make self-expression possible. The common misconception that poets and autists work alone belies the reality that they both often lead lives of substantial connectivity. This is what disability activists have been calling *interdependence*, a state that eschews the isolating and unrealistic expectations of independence to offer a vision for what a richer, more intertwined life might entail.

. . .

In rereading the fourth and final section of Matteo's epic poem, I'm struck by a moment where the main character, who has just encountered his shipmate after a long separation, pauses to wonder how his friend feels. This, my friends, is theory of mind in action. Matteo is duly imagining the emotional cognition of a character who is imagining the emotional cognition of his friend. Matteo is feeling empathy for a character feeling empathy. This wondering shows what we already know, that autistic individuals have always lived and felt and thought empathically. To perceive it readers must engage in creative empathy themselves, which is the lifeblood of all lyrical art forms.

And as long as we're getting creative, let's briefly complicate the underpinnings of theory of mind, which posits "minds" as sharing some kind of mutual neutral understanding. The truth is that theory of mind is far from neutral. It's not the ability to imagine *anyone's* thoughts, but instead represents the highly conditioned ability to imagine the inner world of someone utilizing a particular social framework—a framework that in Baron-Cohen's work we can safely assume belongs to the dominant culture. Here I am reminded of Tito Mukhopadhyay's brilliant satire *Plankton Dreams: What I Learned in Special-Ed*, where he writes:

> I am the scientist who knows why I have autism: to experience the captivity of intellect by one's body and to endure it with absurd aplomb, while others struggle even to fathom such captivity. As a social scientist, I know, however, that nobody is free from captivity. One is captive to one's ego, for example, social obligations, job requirements, et cetera. Which of you neurotypicals is free to sniff a book in public? I have freedom from customary comportment, and as a sniffing scientist, I remain outside the box we term *social norms*. The rest of you purportedly free people are trapped into the social box.[9]

The framework is the box, which, as Tito brilliantly points out, is an enclosure, a trap. It is a transparent trap, rarely revealing its own dimensions to the captive who passively accepts and reproduces it. As Alexis Pauline Gumbs asks, "What are the contours of your captivity?"[10] Or as Sid Ghosh wrote when I shared Tito's quotation with him, "Hapless is one who doesn't see a box." He happened to be wearing a shirt that, to my limited Zoom viewpoint, read, "Think." When his mother, Vaish, moved the laptop back a few inches, I was able to see that it actually read "Think outside the box." Boxes in boxes in boxes.

However well we might be able to perceive the parameters of our boxes, the social box of society requires a further understanding, which is that the enclosure of ableist production is also an enclosure of *speed*. We are conditioned to pace our production at the speed of the machine, a speed that actually *produces* disability, since the human body is forged in multiple ways, with multiple abilities and limits, to inhabit a variety of paces. All but the most "fit" bodies break down under the compulsive, homogenized speed of capital. And if you don't fit, you might be shamed until you do, or rendered invisible.

Of course, this can surface in more subtle ways. When I ask a nonspeaking student a question, I have to consciously downshift from the pace of talking to the pace of typing. And even then, the student might need multiple attempts to find a way their body, in that particular moment, might answer. There might be false starts, sensory interruptions, sudden stimming excitements, or any number of beckonings that divert the student from a simple answer. If I don't move at their pace, always making space for how their body flows into expression, then I might move too quickly toward another tactic, a reframing or an entirely different question. I might dismiss their interest in the original question altogether. And the stakes of that are silence. Erasure. My pace might erase their possibility to contribute. And those stakes go up every time a "troubled abled" person, in the parlance of my student Imane, holds greater potential for the enforcement of power: a teacher, a social worker, an administrator, a police officer. As we've seen far too often over the past few years, the pace of neurodivergence, especially when it intersects with Blackness or other markers of difference, can be a mortal danger.[11]

The trap of the social, which is the trap of the dominant culture—patriarchal, white supremacist, capitalist, carceral—is a trap of hierarchical domination. If theory of mind is inevitably fed by a culture of domination, hierarchy, and exclusion—a culture "expertly" reiterated by the apes of *Planet of the Apes*—then why would anyone, especially a neurodivergent individual, agree to step inside of it?[12] What if we, as neurodivergent individuals, aren't oblivious to this captive formulation of mind, but actively resist it? What if we desire not to compete with others, to judge and order them, but to attend to others with care and curiosity, to reconfigure what sociality might and can mean? And furthermore, what if we desire to attend in more pervasive ways, beyond the limited scope of the human world, dispersing our perceptive warmth in all directions of the animate and inanimate worlds?

To put it plainly, I believe autistic attention is a form of love. Think for a moment of the coercive social system you have been conditioned to accept and replicate. Is that love? In breaking with the social contract we've been born into, in stepping outside the trap of domination, can we make room for other ways of attending to the world? And can poetry be a primary way we wield this mode of attending otherwise? What if we let our poetic, autistic resistance to neurotypical "minding" serve as an opening toward the loving, liberatory worlds we deserve?

. . .

Matteo's poem ends not where the movie ends, but where he decided to end it. Not, as Keats might have had it, with the ironic tragedy of a fallen statue, but with the renewed connection between two friends. Matteo has General Taylor leaving the courtroom, where his intelligence has been on trial, only to see his friend Landon. Matteo truncated his poem at the moment of their reunion, creating a way for these comrades to remain together, while in the film Taylor discovers that Landon has actually been lobotomized.

When Matteo decided that the poem was complete, I told him how much I admired it. While he didn't seem quite as enthusiastic about it as I was, he very well may have been, just in his own way. In any case, he offered that he liked it as well, his eyes fully teeming with that soft focus that made me suspect he was still working the film and text in his head.

We made copies and I took one to Ryan, my face lit with pride and excitement. I really loved Matteo's poem, and I can't stress this enough, *simply for its artistic value.* Remember, I didn't know anything about autism. I'd never heard the term "theory of mind" and I'd never read a single deficit-obsessed paragraph detailing the various challenges inherent to autism. When Ryan read it, he knew Matteo's teachers would want copies.

The next day I came in early and we distributed the stapled pages of Matteo's epic poem. As I watched his teachers read the poem, what I saw left me in a state of disequilibrium. Their faces weren't beaming like mine. They seemed, if anything, nonplussed. Some appeared slightly distraught. Looking back on it now, I imagine each teacher read that poem with a combination of awe and regret. Eventually, there were tears, and not happy ones. Everyone seemed to be avoiding each other's eyes. Like Baron-Cohen's autistic stereotype, I couldn't parse what was happening in the minds of these well-meaning teachers, who were just a moment before laughing and buoyant. It took me years to finally understand, to piece together, through my own experience, what may have transpired.

I believe that in that moment they were really seeing Matteo for the first time. They had walked through an invisible door and gained entry to his planet, invited by the care and complexity of his language. They had seen, all at once, how much more was alive inside him, and how much more of himself he was ready to give. Or maybe it's something they intuited all along and were subconsciously avoiding. Maybe they didn't feel up to the task of nurturing that connection amid all the other complexities of a middle school classroom. My most uncomfortable suspicion, and I'm hesitant to put it in these terms, was that some part of them hadn't actually believed he was fully human.

Far too often, even the best intentioned of us—teachers, parents, peers, experts—forge a crucible of humanness, a misguided test of what it means to be fully human, from the limited materials of our own image. It's impossible to ignore the way Taylor's predicament as "Bright Eyes," a man whose intelligence is deemed, at best, a parlor trick by a collection of so-called professionals, must have resonated with Matteo's own experience. *Planet of the Apes* persists as a cultural touchstone precisely because it questions everything we know about intelligence and otherness. Who is the primate? Who is the primitive? Who will turn our planet into a barren forbidden zone? Who will finally recognize the bright spark of intellect and care emanating from a pair of unlikely eyes?

. . .

This was my first pedagogical experience of autism. Many educators have to navigate a series of pedagogical failures before they find the right approach for working with their autistic students, largely because autistic intelligence and embodiment have been so often misunderstood, underestimated, and generalized by the educational and medical worlds. Matteo's keen perceptions and linguistic gifts were so unexpected by professionals at the time that they may have been ignored, even if he had found opportunities for them to surface. Our success together wasn't a fluke; it was predicated on the reciprocity between poetry and autism, and being a neurodivergent poet myself ensured that I had already researched this field internally for longer than it takes to earn a doctorate. Twenty years later, I find that one of my favorite aspects of running Unrestricted Interest, an organization devoted to neurodivergent listening and languaging, is getting the opportunity to instruct other teachers, whether they are our own teaching-writers or devoted public school teachers or curious personal care assistants (PCAs). Inevitably, someone from the organization I'm partnering with will ask if the training will be useful for teachers with neurotypical students. I love this question, because I know how much my answer might fundamentally change the way they think about education.

If you tailor your lesson plans to an autistic student, you have dramatically expanded the ways those plans can serve neuro-typical students as well. The autistic predilections for play, pattern, and sensory awareness are at the core of human experience, though perhaps with different levels of intensity. Every human body learns through its sensory apparatus and can become overwhelmed by certain kinds of unchecked stimuli. All students deserve the specific attention and care that only an open-thinking educator can provide. Access to education done right doesn't entail a random assortment of accommodations; it finds where our bodies and minds diverge and creates opportunities that are inclusive to them all. If you design an activity—or a classroom, or a dormitory, or a hospital, or a cohousing community—with the needs of autistic people in mind, it will help you better serve all the people who engage with it. Connection, like access, is contagious. If you equip each exceptional student with the opportunities they need to make connections with their peers, you access an exponential likelihood that the class will develop and cultivate a culture of intelligent care.

When those same administrators ask me whether my pedagogy trainings, which focus primarily on poetry, will be useful to teachers of prose, my smile once again turns up with a slightly wicked pleasure. I believe poetry functions like a linguistic headwater, feeding and nurturing every other form of writing with its mineral-rich flow. It is common, for example, to hear an accomplished novelist talk of having first apprenticed at the feet of poetry. But it is rare for a celebrated essayist to suddenly produce a critically lauded book of poems. Countless luminaries have leapt from poetry into the forms that eventually made them famous: James Baldwin, Paul Auster, Michael Ondaatje (and more recently Eula Biss, Ben Lerner, and Eve L. Ewing).

The list goes on and on. Claudia Rankine, the author of *Citizen*, has definitely altered our national conversation about race, in large part by finding a way to suffuse prose with the dynamics and attention of poetry. People who change the landscape of literature are habitually changed by their primary experiences reading and writing poetry.

Despite his critical disregard, I can't tell you how many writers I know first glimpsed the vast possibilities of language by reading e e cummings. For me it was his poem "[Buffalo Bill 's]," which shoots across the page from the titular Bill all the way to Jesus and then contracts back to the almost collegial "Mister Death." In the process, the poem tests our sense of grammatical completeness ("Buffalo Bill 's / defunct . . ." what? Or even who?), sutures words like German compounds ("watersmooth-silver"), and then stops time to let a string of words collide ("onetwothreefourfive pigeonsjustlikethat"). Not to mention cummings's trademark affinity for the lowercase.

What attracts young writers to a poet like cummings is how he expands the world of language. Or, more accurately, the way he reveals all the possibilities of language that we have obscured in our desire for standardized reproduction. Poetry is to prose what dancing is to hiking. Don't get me wrong, I love hiking, but in many ways the trail is the trail. Poetry, on the other hand, can root itself in the moment and spring in unpredictable directions, arms and legs splayed. Which is not to say that poetry is somehow better than prose. The greatest novel and the greatest book of essays and the greatest collection of poems all stand shoulder to shoulder, partaking in the same lush cascade. But I do believe the wellspring found in poetry feeds these other genres in ways they can rarely repay, endowing them with a linguistic momentum that is nearly inexhaustible.

Engaging with poems brings us deeper into our understanding of language, which, in turn, brings us deeper into our understanding of being human. Poetry and autism may seem like perplexing islands far from the mainland of general culture, but what they can teach us about ourselves has the power to bring each of us closer together.

. . .

A couple of years after my formative experience with Matteo, I meet Brian. It is our first day together, a sort of trial-run field trip at the American Museum of Natural History where Brian can feel out my personality and share some of his interests. And I can barely keep up with him. I attempt to keep pace as he flits from display to display, speaking aloud to the taxidermied animals. He warns the dik-dik not to hesitate too long at the Plasticine stream; a sneaky caracal is on the prowl. Moments later he's openly admiring the hippopotamuses, congratulating them on their status as the most lethal African animal. On the move again, he recounts a cheetah's top speed to the hapless ibex calf closely drafting its mother. Twelve-year-old Brian cares about these animals and he cares about their facts. I'd been told he wouldn't (and perhaps couldn't) read, but he has just breezily reeled off hundreds of facts about animals of all shapes and sizes.

After a glorious hour exploring dioramas of African animals we are on our way to the extinct mammals wing. We are walking through the oldest display in the museum, the "North-west Coast Hall," which features artifacts of Native life. As we walk between looming totem poles, Brian grows silent, his face assuming a pained, slightly panicked look. He instinctively brings a cupped hand to each side of his face, blinkering his eyes like a Central Park carriage horse navigating traffic. Is he overwhelmed by the carved faces? Is he reacting to a mysterious sensory trigger I don't perceive? Or is he, as I came to suspect later, protecting himself against the unwelcome reminder that, in addition to animals, the world is also filled with people, who tend to "professionally" categorize one another and make otherness a spectacle?

The following day, when we sit down to work together for the first time, Brian is quick to set the terms: "You can teach me, but I don't want to talk about people or anything made up." Brian's deal-breakers pose a significant pedagogical problem for me, as I've been tasked with teaching him literature, a subject that principally constructs its edifice from the bricks of people and the mortar of the made-up. But I don't say any of that. I say, "Let's talk about what you *do* want to talk about."

· · ·

In my own Netflix-facilitated animal research, I'd come across a video series called *Walking with Prehistoric Beasts*. It's a CGI nature documentary about largely forgotten mammal species that existed between sixty-five million years ago, when the large dinosaurs disappeared, and thirty thousand years ago, when Neanderthal tribes and other early hominids roamed the

Earth. The show uses paleontological evidence from the fossil record to reconstruct several different time periods and the nearly unthinkable mammals that inhabited them. Twenty-five million years ago, your still-tiny mammal ancestor might find itself needing to scurry between an entelodont (a sort of warthog the size of an SUV) and a twenty-ton indricothere (a creature with the morphology of a giraffe and the texture of a rhinoceros).

Brian loves it from the opening credits. He even records the theme music and listens to it on his iPod. And since the video series has been made by humans who cannot help but tell stories, the episodes organically give rise to questions of a literary nature. After the first episode I ask Brian who the good guys (*Leptictidium*) and bad guys (*Gastornis*) are. After the second I ask him to identify the protagonist (*Basilosaurus*) and antagonist (*Andrewsarchus*), noting that the *Basilosaurus* makes a complex protagonist given that it is a predatory whale. After episode three we delve into neutral characters (*Cynodictis*) that move the plot along and begin writing speculative dialogues between competing creatures (*Paraceratherium* and *Hyaenodon*), who often turn out to be much more collaborative than you'd expect. By episode four our hominid ancestor *Australopithecus* has arrived, and Brian, who has previously held a staunch humans-are-not-mammals policy, begins to waver slightly, intrigued by this odd middle ground of personhood he watches lumber in and out of the frame. Soon we are writing dialogues between Cro-Magnon man and the mighty *Megaloceros*. Brian's begrudging acknowledgment of humans' mammal status has softened into genuine interest. When the series is complete, he even agrees to watch the sequel: *Walking with Cavemen*.

• • •

It has taken roughly a month and many prehistoric beasts, but Brian's aversion to exploring the subject of people has modified into something like guarded curiosity, a transformation made possible by reveling together in his "restricted interest" and exploring how it might lead to adjacent territory. When you first meet a new neurotypical student, it can sometimes take quite a while before they reveal (or realize) their passions. But students on the spectrum are open and generous with their passions. It usually takes no more than five minutes to discover their area of devoted study. This is their island. If you're Matteo, the island is *Planet of the Apes*; if you're Brian, it's the taxonomical class of Mammalia. Either way, it's a vertical endeavor, deeply researched, and seemingly unconnected to the landmasses floating around it.

The magical thing about islands, however, is that they aren't truly floating. If you can follow an island down to its root, under the waters, you'll find it's connected to everything around it. *Planet of the Apes* is a cultural touchstone because its concerns and ideas remain salient for all of us. What does it feel like to be doubted, to be different? Who gets to decide the shape of intelligence or the value of a living thing? And what separates human from animal, or delineates the animal from inside the human? When you take the time to study these islands alongside autistic thinkers, your complementary vision may be able to gradually see archipelagic sister islands streaming off in all directions. Traveling alongside a neurodivergent student on that journey, wayfinding from their island outward, can transform both of your abilities to understand new subject areas and connect to the people around you, who inevitably take notice.

. . .

Though people are now a welcome topic, Brian and I are still only halfway to literature. My instinct is to complicate the notion of "made up." Given Brian's burgeoning curiosity about middle grounds and missing links, a curiosity I immediately connect to Matteo's, I decide to introduce him to the world of cryptozoology. Cryptological creatures are the denizens of our imagination and, sometimes, our nightmares: Big Foot, the New Jersey Devil, Chupacabra, and the Loch Ness Monster. Are these creatures made up, misidentified, or simply unsubstantiated? In any case, Brian is all in. Our studies dovetail nicely with geography and global cultures. Brian is especially drawn to Big Foot, perhaps because it represents a variation on the hominids we've just delved into, a sort of hybrid with one (very large) foot in the world of primates and the other in the world of humankind.

Brian becomes so attached to these cryptozoological cousins that he undertakes an epistolary challenge over the holiday break, writing a series of letters back and forth from one cousin to another. Earnest questions carom in literary form between the northern Sasquatch and southern Skunk Ape, between the Himalayan Yeti and the Australian Yowie. These cousins talk about what it feels like to be outcasts. They commiserate over the senseless cruelties of humankind. They promise to visit soon.

. . .

I recall these letters when, two years later, we begin reading *A Wrinkle in Time*. Fourteen-year-old Brian is no longer troubled by the kinds of imaginative leaps Madeleine L'Engle takes in her young adult classic, but he is suddenly pained to recognize himself in the struggles of its main character, Meg. While one might expect him to identify with Charles, one of the only spectrum-like characters of that literary era, his affinity for Meg speaks to her and Brian's shared difficulty fitting into neurotypical social milieus. Charles is the stereotypical savant type, a deeply exceptional person for whom normality is not an expectation or even desire. Brian is drawn to Meg's more commonplace turmoil, perched somewhere on the edge of normal, looking down with a mixture of yearning and aversion.

Brian has just recently become aware that he is on the spectrum. Over the summer his parents told him he had Asperger syndrome,[13] and he's been reading a book by Luke Jackson, a spectrum teen, called *Freaks, Geeks, and Asperger Syndrome: A User Guide to Adolescence.* If it weren't for his newfound identity or the crucial contextualizing of this book, I wonder whether Brian would have recognized himself in Meg. In questioning who he himself is, he is able to ask more nuanced questions about who other people are, and how he might relate to them.

Attempting to build on Brian's emotional connection to the story, I suggest we annotate the novel, glossing each moment where Brian feels a sense of kinship with one of the characters. He agrees and decides to call it *The Spectrum Kids' Guide to A Wrinkle in Time.* Here are Brian's first three entries:

On page 7, Meg says, "It's the weather on top of everything else. On top of me. On top of Meg Murray doing everything wrong." No one is always perfect, but when you are a kid on the Spectrum you make more mistakes mostly. It makes you feel bad to make mistakes, but it teaches you something.

Page 10 has Meg talking to her cat, "Just be glad you're a kitten and not a monster like me." Nobody is really a monster. If you get so frustrated, it makes you look like a monster and feel like one too. This is when you feel out of control. Everyone feels this way sometimes, but Spectrum kids feel this way more often.

On page 11, Meg is thinking about her twin brothers, Sandy and Dennys: "The twins didn't have any problems. They weren't great students, but they weren't bad students either." Not everybody is "normal." Very few people are normal and it's boring. The things that keep people from being normal—the way they look or act—are the things that make them different or special.

You can see that Brian is learning how to own his own difference, his "quirkiness," and translate it from "wrong" to "special." He's speaking to his own feelings of monstrosity, giving them light and shelter. He's coaching himself on how to transform mistakes into opportunities, before they become emotionally debilitating. And he's doing all of this by productively identifying with a made-up human!

On page 32 Meg says, "I do face facts. They're lots easier to face than people, I can tell you." Kids on the Spectrum do like facts. Often they memorize the facts about something they like to tell people. Facts always stay the same, but people are always changing.

It may have taken years, but Brian learned to see how his glorious and insulated realm of Mammalia connected to myriad islands in all directions. And these years were not a slog. We invented poem forms like the Diprotodon Double Acrostic. Brian wrote an origin story for King Kong that involved an Indonesian *Gigantopithecus* crossing a prehistoric land bridge. He created a personalized audio tour of the Museum of Natural History that included its newly opened "Human Origins" exhibit.

By witnessing the depths of Brian's island, we developed a mutual trust, and we found organic ways to dive down together. Then we traced the ocean floor, moving at Brian's unique pace toward one fascinating landmass after another. More than a dozen years later, Brian and I are still good friends. He recently graduated college, and we still exchange messages, movie suggestions, and factoids about the natural world. Although we live far apart, we find a way to connect, and we often reflect back on the magic of our time together—a time that was formative for us both. The other day I mentioned that he might like a new film called *Wolfwalkers*, which features a more positive, Celtic take on the melding of wolf and, in this case, woman. He wrote back in rhyme, "I will see anything you recommend because you're my good old friend."

The Moon Is Especially Full

Two Wide Open Eyes—The Moon Is Full of Love—Full of Caffeine—Our Lives Exceed Transaction—Creative Reading—The Moon Is Laughing—Underestimated and Undermined—We Are All a Star—Reluctant Suns—I Find Buzzing

On the eve of the Strawberry Moon, I asked Zach to look at the word "MOON," all caps, and tell me what he noticed. With the help of his communication partner, Lindsee, Zach slowly and deliberately hit the *O* key on his keyboard twice. "That's what I see, too," I said, our eyes meeting and not meeting across the virtual interface of Skype. MOON: two wide-open eyes flanked by the erect, owlish ears of *M* and *N*. "Tonight," I continued, "everyone will be looking up at the Strawberry Moon, but I wonder, what would the moon see if it was looking back?"

Professionals are often focused on assuaging feelings of isolation among neurodivergent thinkers, and while these may exist, sometimes acutely, other times I've found those feelings to be more of a projection than anything else. Often those same professionals miss signs of connection that others may find self-evident. Over nearly twenty years, every neurodivergent student I've worked with has lived a richly social existence. I constantly marvel at the way nonspeaking spellers and typers constellate their own complex systems of friendship and support, fostering communities of mutual regard wherever they go. Part of my work as an educator is to give students the tools they need to see possibilities for connection with others, but just as often I'm drawn to poems that give students the tools they need to help *me* see the complex web of connections they are carefully nurturing every day.

Zach, a twenty-one-year-old nonspeaking typer, struggles mightily with fine motor skills, including the use of his voice, which he cannot sufficiently organize into speech. As Tito Mukhopadhyay writes, referring to himself in the third-person: "The problem with autism was making him feel that his voice was a distant substance that was required to be collected and put somewhere inside his throat. But he was unable to find it. He wept for it."[1] The fine motor movements of the throat and tongue, which most of us take for granted, are not available to Zach, and his voice emerges only through typing, which he has worked incredibly hard to access. In order to find his typing arm, Zach requires a consistent form of resistance, which also helps to minimize erratic movements and allow his index finger a chance to find its mark. Proprioception is the key here. This is one reason autists profess a love of the ocean, where the water's density and current's pull give them constant proprioceptive input. Or as Adam puts it: "The weight of water opens my ability to swan dive into the world of sense . . . The weight of water lands the body that I sometimes cannot feel, and support is also helping me land this language."[2]

Lindsee, Zach's support today, does not move him toward the letters but actually pulls his wrist away from the keys. That motion creates the input Zach needs to find a neutral beginning to his motor movements and feel his own way forward. It's not coincidental to me that poetry often arises from constraint, the way the rules of a sonnet or haiku provide a generative opposing force to the mind of the writer, focusing the way language can carry thought.

In this way, poetic structure can afford students like Zach greater opportunity to connect with the way language, *their* language, is moving on the page. When a writer is just starting out and searching for a way to connect with their language, the exterior scaffolding of form might be more elaborate. As a student gains facility as a typer or poet or both, they can choose to keep or remove these scaffolds. They might find the form itself to be a passion, as many of my students do. Or they may develop a connection to language that prefers to flow free. The scaffold of Zach's poem would be the moon's gaze, making its tidal tug.

I set up the first line, "I see the moon and the moon sees _____," writing it on a Google Doc both Zach and I could see at once, magical letters emerging in oracular fashion across the screen of his iPad. I was in Minneapolis and he was in Carbondale, Colorado, but we'd both be under the Strawberry Moon later that night. Zach's face tightened into a grimace of concentration as he typed: "p . . . e . . . o . . . p . . . l . . . e." I read the line out loud, "I see the moon and the moon sees people," before silently typing in the next line: "The moon is full of _____." Again, Zach's placid, attentive expression became transformed by the labor of each letter: "l . . . o . . . v . . . e." My heart, as it often did in Zach's company, abruptly lightened. I read the stanza aloud: "I see the moon and the moon sees people / The moon is full of love." While Lindsee and I outwardly beamed, Zach angled his head and looked off into the distance with calm focus, like someone attempting to decipher a faint and curious sound.

We repeated the structure for the second stanza: "I see the moon and the moon sees blue and green / The moon is full of bugs." The moon, in its looking, has pivoted from people to insects, from love to bugs. Zach, whose challenges divert him from accurately producing the sound of words with his mouth, captured and carried the sonic texture of those same words through his typing. In rhyming love and bugs, Zach created a winning and comical slant rhyme, reminding me of Emily Dickinson. This created a delightful image in my mind, the moon's loveful buzzing held aloft by countless blue and green wings.

Zach's third stanza continued where the second left off: "I see the moon and the moon sees purple gold red / The moon is full of stars." Love, which is often said to feel like butterflies, had become bugs, and those insects turned out to be lightning bugs, a panoply of multicolored stars filling the moon's expectant belly. I was expecting another slant rhyme to finish out the poem, but Zach had a more drastic curveball in mind.

After I placed the first line ("I see the moon and the moon sees _____") into our Google Doc, Lindsee rerouted the cursor on Zach's screen and he typed "b . . . i . . . l . . . l." Bill's restive body had been orbiting Zach's desk during our Skype session, inconstantly popping in and out of the frame. Zach and Bill are not only classmates, but they are also housemates in an historic home in downtown Carbondale renovated to suit the needs of neurodivergent residents, complete with quiet LED lighting, radiant heat, and a profusion of beanbag chairs. This kind of sensory friendly architecture is on the rise, and you can now find "sensory-inclusion rooms" in even the largest of public spaces, like basketball arenas and airports.

Zach and Bill spend nearly every day together, engaging life alongside one another in classrooms, coffee shops, and the natural beauty of the Rocky Mountains. And through all the days and years they've spent together, despite their intimate and amiable companionship, they might never share what neurotypicals presume is a "normal" conversation. In fact, someone unfamiliar with them (and unfamiliar with autism) might erroneously conclude that Zach and Bill barely take note of one another.

But that's where poetry comes in. Not only is poetry a crucial platform for exploring and expressing how we live and feel, but it can also function as a means to communicate what we perceive in others, to nurture connection and make the connections we already have more fully known. I set up the final line of the poem, "The moon is full of _____," and Zach, now smiling broadly, typed, "c . . . a . . . f . . . f . . . e . . . i . . . n . . . e." Both Lindsee and I burst out laughing, and Zach made a particular high-pitched humming noise that signaled he was likewise delighted. Bill, who may or may not have been paying attention to Zach's composition, continued to pace the room, bouncing slightly on his muscular calves. Knowing that part of Bill and Zach's day was spent perfecting the social exchange of buying a drink at the coffee shop downtown, I asked Lindsee if the constantly moving Bill was given to drinking anything with caffeine in it, and she said, definitively, "No way."

Zach's observation was not only witty and sophisticated, but in my view, it was also gloriously metaphorical. Stars and caffeine possess a slant logic of energy to connect them, a twinkling electric buzz like neurons bolstered by caffeine. In this poem it's instantly clear how much Zach sees and knows of Bill. They might not share normative conversations, but through poetry Bill and Zach can engage on levels that are much deeper.

Nonspeaking autistic artist and elder Larry Bissonnette achieved what he winkingly calls "popular autistic celebrity" alongside his friend Tracy Thresher in the film *Wretches & Jabberers*.[3] Reflecting on the film and his experience, he writes, "Toward educating others about most hard to understand concept of presuming the competence of people without ordered for real intelligent conversation speech, the film has been perfect learning by observation of real people tool."[4] So often professionals and laypeople link competence to a seemly performance of seemingly intelligent "conversation speech." But the way it is "ordered" can be both a grammatical constraint and a prepackaging of language that strips it of its character, autistic or otherwise. So while transactional exchanges may play an important role in the business of society, autistic exchanges, like the ones found throughout *Wretches & Jabberers*, can dramatically expand conceptions of intelligence that have been direly limited by the hegemony of (pre) ordered professional languagings. Like Larry and Tracy, Zach and Bill live lives of enmeshed sociability and intelligence. A poem has the potential to communicate the parts of our lives that exceed transaction, parts that often occur unspoken until they encounter a form, an invitation, an occasion of voice.

· · ·

One way I like to facilitate and encourage these deeper conversations is to share poem forms between students. The passing of the form is like a handshake, a kind of intimate greeting, but it also functions like a question. It asks, "How would *you* respond?" or "How might this kind of poem help bring some specific part of you out into the light?" When someone writes a sonnet, they may be conversing with Petrarch or Shakespeare (who was conversing with Petrarch) or Ted Berrigan (who was conversing with Shakespeare conversing with Petrarch) or Sandra Simonds (who was conversing with Berrigan conversing with Shakespeare conversing with Petrarch). Sometimes stepping into another person's poem form is like stepping inside their mind (and all the minds they stepped into); you notice how the contours of their choices resonate with or diverge from yours. In essence, it weds creative writing with creative reading, adopting and adapting the literature of another to communicate one's own experience. It allows autistic writers to practice artistic and social literacy at the same time, invigorating pathways in both directions.

. . .

A few years after Zach wrote his moon poem, I found myself working with a group of young adult writers in Mark's classroom at the South Education Center. By then, Mark and I had worked extensively in one-on-one sessions, and his burgeoning poetic abilities had dramatically transformed his classroom and the expectations of his peers. On this particular day, Mark was especially excited to bring his fellow nonspeaking typer Daniel into the fold. Daniel is a classmate whom I'd invited to write with us on many occasions, reassured by Mark that his quiet demurrals were only evidence that it wasn't the right moment.

With Zach's keen observation of Bill in mind, I built a version of the "mOOn" poem that could work collaboratively to reveal multiple relationships. In the first stanzas I asked the students to self-reflect, and in the subsequent stanzas I asked them to turn the moon's gaze on someone else in the classroom.

I began with Khalil, a soft-spoken young man with a penchant for listening to Prince. Though Khalil speaks, he does not offer unprompted spoken communication. His language arises in response to questions, which makes a highly scaffolded poem a good fit. I asked him what the moon would grow full with if it were looking at him. He answered, "Calm."

The atmosphere in the classroom was indeed calm, though I'd been told it had been a rocky afternoon and I shouldn't expect the students to be calm enough to write anything during our session. Mark's teacher Katie often remarked on this phenomenon. Days when I was to visit their classroom were tumultuous, perhaps *because* I was visiting. Was it excitement, anxiety, a marshaling of resources toward writing? Whatever the cause, and it may have been different for each student, Katie noticed that minutes before I was to arrive, a kind of buzzing and contagious equanimity would settle over the class. Often Khalil would be reclining on a mat with his headphones on, returning to "Purple Rain" when I walked through the door.

Next came Mark, who was particularly animated. I could tell that he was thrilled about the participation of Daniel. Mark himself told me several times that Daniel could and would write, so I was feeling optimistic. It had been a year since I'd first started working with Mark, and he had become very adept at recognizing and subverting the forms I suggested. He typed:

I see the moon
and the moon sees Mark
the moon is laughing
at an asteroid looking
at me

I'd asked the class to self-reflect, and Mark had complicated that self-reflection through a third party: the moon looking at an asteroid looking at him. It can easily be read as a meta-commentary about Mark's own role in bringing Daniel into expression. He'd been conspiring to triangulate the three of us for several weeks, and now it was finally happening, with Khalil joining the mix as well. He was setting the stage for Daniel, whom he'd been encouraging toward self-advocacy. This was a fundamental aspect of their relationship—typing back and forth about the systemic challenges of a nonspeaking life inside public and private institutions, where someone is always watching over you, often with the unfounded presumption that your unique corporeal experience is synonymous with (or proof of) a meager intellectual capacity.

Daniel, whose time had been routinely and savagely wasted by a system demanding proof of his cognitive vigor in ways his body couldn't navigate, wasn't going to waste any time in speaking out. He wrote:

I see the moon
and the moon sees Daniel
the moon is especially full
of less testing
of our intelligence

An excoriating combination of rhetoric and lyricism. What I love most about this stanza—which I have to remind myself was the first one Daniel had ever written in my presence—is the cascade of short *E* sounds—especially, less, testing, intelligence—all packed into a single short phrase. I also love how Daniel chooses the pronoun "our," which enlarges his indictment to include not only his classmates, but all the non-speaking autists out there suffering the indignity of misguided testing. Perhaps the "we" implied by Daniel's "our" includes all the neurodivergent people who have been underestimated and undermined.

It was clear that Mark felt seen and spoken for. He was clapping the insides of his wrists together and smiling brightly, bouncing a little in his seat. I could tell he wanted to respond. With Katie's assistance, he steadied his excitement enough to type: "I see the moon / and the moon sees Daniel / the moon is full of pride." What a joy it is to be in a classroom where students like Daniel and Mark are beaming, where they not only feel seen, but feel heard as well.

In my experience, I feel the most human when I bring some part of myself out into the open, where I can be known and valued. I wondered how many hours and days and even years Daniel and Mark had spent waiting for the full scope of their humanity to be grasped by more than a handful of family and a few teachers. Daniel was ready to write because Mark and Katie had persuaded him that I would create a safe space for his expression. I was here because Katie had come to a talk I gave at a local library. She advocated for me to give the same talk at her school. That led to a month-long residency, which finally led to her classroom, where she sensed Mark's and Daniel's yearning to be heard. That led to a year of discovery with Mark and, finally, to this day, when Daniel, who had been so wary to participate, finally risked the vulnerability of making himself seen and heard, of bringing a rightfully indignant part of himself out into the open. Week after week, Mark kept typing messages to him. "Chris knows you are intelligent." "Chris doesn't doubt you." "I will help you." And all his and Katie's perseverance had finally paid off.

Khalil, swept up in the resplendence of the moment, wrote:

> I see the moon
> and the moon sees Mark
> the moon is full
> with the bright light
> of six stars

Why six stars? I didn't ask Khalil in the moment, though I wish I had. Especially since the specificity of those six keeps standing out to me. Three other students were missing or unable to participate that day. Perhaps it was the full retinue of the classroom, Khalil knowing how much Mark desires a community of inclusion. Or it could simply mean that Mark and Khalil and Daniel possess a resplendent glow—their six eyes shining—that is best captured in multiplicity and alliteration. Interpretation is left up to the reader, though I do want to bring in an additional reference point here: Prince's song "Baby I'm a Star," which you can find on his most famous (and Khalil's most favorite) album, *Purple Rain*.

The chorus of "Baby I'm a Star" describes an as-yet-unacknowledged star who is eager to shine among collective constellations. Prince even uses the curious construction "I are" to indicate his own inherent multiplicity.

Not only is Prince multiple, but so *are* each of us. Identity doesn't consist of a single point, but a complicated multiplicity of points. The writers of this poem could be variously described as autists, poets, Prince enthusiasts, disability activists, students, immigrants, survivors, leaders, lovers, beloveds, and people of color. And in Prince's song we are all, in our glorious and interconnected discrepancy, stellar; we are all part of the same star.

Daniel brought the poem full circle in his final stanza, reasserting his previous claim through a look at Khalil:

I see the moon
and the moon sees Khalil
the moon is sad
about testing his intelligence

In speaking of autistic people, it is always crucial to emphasize the vast difference among them. Though they share the same classroom, Daniel and Khalil do not share the same challenges. Khalil, though minimally expressive, has an audible voice with which to answer direct questions. He has significant sensorimotor challenges, but they pale in comparison to Daniel's. Nonetheless, Daniel is here asserting that their plight is the same. Khalil's ability to speak doesn't protect him from prejudice, and it certainly doesn't exempt him from the indignities of neurotypically designed one-size-fits-all testing.

And, in fact, no one is exempt from those indignities, even and especially the teachers. I read Daniel's sad moon as a stand-in for Katie and for all teachers who are required to administer tests they know don't accurately reflect the intelligence and vibrancy of their students.

The moon alone can't make light. It can only catch and reflect what the sun gives it. The moon is receptive and reflective. Great educators often function like the moon; they find the right angle to best reflect reluctant suns. Students like Mark, having claimed the mantle of expression, do their best to shine what they can from their peers. Teachers like Katie search tirelessly for the right conditions, the proper alignment that can allow their students' bright lights to be seen. And sometimes students seek out a willing sun that can illuminate their true faces, not a perpetually new and meager grin, but a waxing orb ready to burst open. State-obligated tests have proved to be a poor and prejudiced option. They occlude, in equal measure, both the student's radiance and the teacher's luminosity, blocking whatever rich and responsive faculties each might otherwise shine forth. As we move further into this new millennium, the neurodiversity movement is changing the way we think about difference and ability. Its light, bright with the contributions of young writers like Khalil, Mark, and Daniel, is growing especially full.

The Moon Sees Me

I see the moon
and the moon sees Khalil
the moon is full of calm

I see the moon
and the moon sees Mark
the moon is laughing
at an asteroid looking
at me

I see the moon
and the moon sees Daniel
the moon is especially full
of less testing
of our intelligence

I see the moon
and the moon sees Daniel
the moon is full of pride

I see the moon
and the moon sees Mark
the moon is full
with the bright light
of six stars

I see the moon
and the moon sees Khalil
the moon is sad
about testing his intelligence

The illuminative potential of this poem form is still going strong. At the time of this writing, I have witnessed more than fifty different poets take the moon like a baton and carry it into unexpected territories. As a teacher, I can honestly say it's been far more useful to me than the acrostic, that classroom classic where you spell out a word with the first letter of each line. And it isn't the only student poem I've seen gather this sort of inter-subjective momentum. That's one of the more fulfilling aspects of teaching the way I do, trusting in the combined resourceful-ness I find buzzing between my students and me. The patterns they create become an open-source technology for others, and it's a joy to watch as they morph and grow along the way.

The Listening World

Back to Natural—Bird's-Eye Poem—A Manifold of
Complementary Thinkers—A More-Than-Human World—
Every Flapping Form—A Dense Dance—Into Silence
and Humming—The Animal Trying to Bite You—A
Spontaneous Garden—A Thriving, Wild Chorus

I never could have imagined writing this book during a pandemic. The quietness I experience regularly in my sessions with nonspeaking students has spread itself onto the streets, as if the calm dominion of night has been allowed to hold court twenty-four hours a day. With my three-year-old boy and his seven-year-old brother crashing and careening about, however, the house is anything but quiet—except for this particular hour, nap time, when the youngest sleeps and the older one slogs through his first-grade distance learning, affording me the space I need to catch each of Mark's words as Indu relays them over our Zoom chat, Max listening beyond the door, ready to edit once our session is over.

Mark types: "We will not get back to normal. We will only get back to natural." Living in Minneapolis, I am graced with a slew of regional parks and nature centers within a short drive of our home. As I spend more and more of this unthinkable time in the woods with my children, listening and looking and building and playing in more-than-human milieus, those words leaven my hopes. No, the normal has not served us. When we return to whatever aspects of our lives remain from before COVID-19's arrival, our perceptions will be both sharpened and softened, keen and patient in ways that might help us better navigate future uncertainty. As so many of us are forced to learn how to stop barreling through the world, we are growing gradually more awake, our senses more alive to the world around us. We are reaching into a space where neurodivergent thinkers live every day.

. . .

Bill and I were staring at a red-tailed hawk at the Hallam Lake Nature Preserve in Aspen, Colorado. The hawk, which appeared to be returning our stare, had been rendered flightless by a traumatic injury. Having suffered through a number of health issues over the previous few years, I projected my own weariness on the hawk, but Bill, whom you met in the last chapter, was bouncing restlessly on his feet, ever-spry. A ruggedly handsome devotee of outdoor life in the Roaring Fork Valley, Bill spent his days climbing and biking and skiing. He looked cut out of a Patagonia catalogue. And it was readily apparent to me that at twenty-eight years old, with his bulging calves and wiry forearms, Bill was in better shape than I had ever been or would be.

The label "autistic" can lead some to imagine Bill lacks certain intrinsic capacities that others take for granted, including empathy and linguistic aptitude. To the least initiated eye, these assumptions might seem justified by Bill's actions—he flaps his hands, eschews eye contact, seems disengaged from the fluid back-and-forth of neurotypical conversation, and finds mundane tasks like buying breakfast at the local coffee shop to be a challenge. On this particular day, however, Bill will use his keen perceptions, made keener by autism, to cut cleanly through the wall of false assumptions.

When we first arrived at the red-tailed hawk's enclosure, our guide informed us how the raptor had become a resident of Hallam Lake, having fractured its ulna. Bill jumped up and down with a passionate moan. Though he does communicate verbally, Bill appeared too pained by the information to express his empathy in words, but perhaps the writing exercise I had prepared would help bring his feelings to light.

We were joined by an assortment of staff from Ascendigo, a Carbondale-based nonprofit serving the autistic community through a rigorous mix of outdoor activities, sports, life skills, employment opportunities, and, increasingly, intellectual enrichment like creative writing. I asked Bill and his peers to pick one of the three protected raptors and study it closely, paying close attention to what the bird hears and sees. I called this challenge a "bird's-eye" poem and wanted them to communicate the experience of a bird from the inside out. Since Bill often finds the motor process of writing difficult, his occupational therapist began by asking some generative questions. When she asked Bill what the hawk might be looking at, he replied "Me." When she asked Bill what the hawk feels when it looks at him, he replied "Happy." I asked him how he knew that the hawk was feeling happy and he said, "The hawk is smiling at me." I typed up the first few lines on my laptop and asked Bill if he wanted to change anything; he shook his head.

At first, his responses appear to confirm an autistic world-view, going back to the etymological root of autism: self-focused. The hawk even takes on an anthropomorphic smile. I asked Bill to observe the hawk further and tell me what he saw. It's here that the poem gradually transformed, allowing the bird's own experience to come into the foreground: "He spreads his wings / He scratches his feathers."

Notice the shift in address from "the hawk" to "he," demonstrating the autistic penchant for personification, a common poetic trope, but even more common among autistic people, revealing an inclination toward warmhearted inclusivity. Autistic thinkers welcome the participation of animals, trees, objects, and even weather into our human world of thought and action.

Neurotypical brains, which prioritize human content, zero in on the complex dance of social life constantly unfolding, alert at all times to a change in the established social choreography. Great poets, however, must ground their work in sensory observations that move past the often transactional nature of human experiences to get at the vaster, more-than-human dance going on all around. Caught up in daily rush, it's easy to overlook the more subtle exchanges transpiring. And that's what many autistic writers do naturally.

Bill returned to his poem, driven to finish it:

The hawk hears rustling leaves
The hawk wants to fly
so he hears

For someone said to have profound language challenges, a word like "rustling" is remarkably apt; it sets the scene for a lovely aural trio linking the *L* sounds of rustling, leaves, and fly. These subtle choices drew me closer to the thrall of the poem. I asked Bill to complete the final line. His therapist wondered aloud what the hawk might be hearing. To our ears the sentence needed its final noun, but Bill saw (or heard) it differently. Despite our prodding, he repeatedly indicated that the poem was complete.

I stood next to him, watching the hawk tilt its head upward, searching the trees and the sky beyond them, shifting focus to listen to an airplane in the distance. That's when I realized that Bill *had* successfully adopted the bird's-eye (or ear) view. And that he had brought me along with him. The poem was finished precisely *because* the hawk had a broken wing. He couldn't fly out to meet these sounds and sights, as much as he clearly desired to do so. He could only *hear* flight as it was embodied by distant airplanes and other birds. Not only was the poem complete, but through its seeming incompleteness Bill was able to offer a more nuanced reflection of the life of this disabled bird.

Bill's insight allows the reader to restage the so-called social deficit of autism by showing how it belies an ethical strength, like attending equally to all facets of the environment, enlarging what we care for and about. We often demand that autists learn how to act more like "us," some specious version of normal. But what if we spent more time trying to understand how each individual voice, precisely because it is different, might contribute to a larger and more invigorating conversation about who "we" are and how we're changing to meet an increasingly complex and diverse world?

When we think of unique and caring individuals like Bill as a collection of deficits, we not only risk alienating them, but we also risk jeopardizing the parts of ourselves that necessarily exist outside the so-called norm. In life, as in poetry, it's best to remain open and assume ability, so you can learn alongside perceptive listeners like Bill who hear the hurt and yearning of a more-than-human world. Together, as a manifold of complementary thinkers, we can begin to cultivate the rich, layered, and autistic attention our planet desperately needs.

. . .

For years now I've lived with that multihyphenate phrase careening in and between my ears: *a more-than-human world*. Cultural ecologist David Abram used it to anchor the subtitle of his book *The Spell of the Sensuous: Perception and Language in a More-Than-Human World*, a book that has served as my own anchor for several years. The book is a story of how our language practice as human beings began firmly rooted—through sound and symbol—in the natural world and then was gradually severed from that natural connection. Linguistic forms like poetry serve as a counterforce to that severing, in that they reconnect language with its sensual foundations. And the more that poetry can be engaged with the larger chorus of animate voice, the better it can fulfill that recuperative role.

The notion of a world that is explicitly more-than-human can seem at once obvious and fussy. Of course we live in a world that encompasses more-than-human affairs, but we're taught that what exists beyond those affairs is somehow ancillary to the "real world" of daily needs, responsibilities, and desires. The "real world" is characterized by adult realities and compromising hierarchies in which we must know our place. As Dara McAnulty writes: "My childhood, although wonderful, is still confined. I'm not free. Daily life is all busy roads and lots of people. Schedules, expectations, stress."[1] It's a claustrophobic and often entirely unreal space in which many of us are learning to dwell less and less these days.

A more-than-human world, on the other hand, invites us to reconsider our relationship to, well . . . relationships. "Humans are tuned for relationship," Abram writes. "The eyes, the skin, the tongue, ears, and nostrils—all are gates where our body receives the nourishment of otherness. . . . For the largest part of our species' existence, humans have negotiated relationships with every aspect of the sensuous surroundings, exchanging possibilities with every flapping form, with each textured surface and shivering entity that we happened to focus on."[2] It pleases me greatly to find "every flapping form" within this quotation. In my years as a teacher of neurodivergent students, I have encountered many flapping forms and have learned to better recognize the subtle self-stimulating behaviors—toes dancing in anticipation, knee's silent jackhammer, a rhythmic pressure applied to the fingertips—that regularly arise in my own body.

In an age that is increasingly out of focus or focused more and more on tiny screens overflowing with human news, our ability to encounter a lived experience of otherness—a muskrat surfacing near a storm drain, the pallor of leaves sickened by rust fungus, a miniscule monarch egg clinging to the underside of a milkweed leaf—dwindles, and so does our ability to understand ourselves. Abram goes on to write, "We are human only in contact, and conviviality, with what is not human."[3]

Autistic thinkers have prodigious gifts for perception and passion. And often these twin gifts are directed toward the more-than-human world in ways that transform our society for the better. There is, of course, the example of Temple Grandin, author of *Animals in Translation*, who has written at length about the relationship between humans and animals.[4] There is also Greta Thunberg, who uses her passionate, no-nonsense speeches to wake us from the "real world" so we can see with clear eyes the more-than-human world in front of us that must be saved, even if only to save ourselves. And most recently there is McAnulty himself, his keen observations allowing us to revel alongside him in the intimate, interconnected wonder of the Northern Irish landscape and beyond.

Autistic thinkers habitually see and hear with an environmental bandwidth that far exceeds their neurotypical counterparts. They perceive widely, warmly, and with an earnest curiosity that treats the more-than-human world as a phenomenal network to be engaged, not a menu of resources to be exploited. Although many autistic thinkers like Grandin, or Brian from Chapter 2, are fascinated with mammals, the scope of autistic attention doesn't end there. It doesn't even limit itself to the kingdoms of Animalia or Plantae. Mark has written to me of his argumentative gut flora and the rousing inner life of rocks. When Tito writes about miners trapped underground, he finds himself thinking of the oxygen molecules themselves. Adam thinks about the endlessly variable movement of water and the grounding of sticks, wielding his body like a blood-filled dowsing rod to maneuver through a teeming, animated landscape. Where some perceive nothing but a mute backdrop to their busy human affairs, these autistic thinkers comprehend a bustling chorus of more-than-human voices accompanied by a dense dance of more-than-human forms.

Simply put, they find meaning in the environment. And without this particular form of meaning, suffused with "the nourishment of otherness," our understanding of what it means to be human threatens to become increasingly flattened under our surface obsession with human affairs. It's a paradox of the contemporary world: we have grown so adept at studying ourselves that we have forgotten who we are. We have become trapped in what neurologists refer to as our default mode network, a system of brain activity that is inherently self-focused. And while autism etymologically means self-focused, autists actually spend far less time in this default mode network than their neurotypical peers.[5] Although this can give them the appearance of social impairment, it can also signal a tendency to think beyond the narrow duality of self/other understandings of the world. In my experience, autists often inhabit cognitive and even corporeal spaces of inseparability with the world around them. In other words, the "oneness" with everything that so many mystics doggedly seek is a feeling with which many autists are intimately familiar.

Bill reminded me how language, in small and subtle ways, can nourish our understanding of otherness, loosening the binds of the "real world" to better enter the lyrical animal ecosystem of thinking beneath it. When I began working with Hannah

Emerson, I needed no more than one session to recognize I'd found a new mentor in perceiving and articulating the conviviality of natural forms.

. . .

From the moment Hannah appears on the computer screen she is singing. It's not the kind of singing you find in a karaoke bar, but the kind you find in the woods—a complex series of repetitive trills pouring forth from the syrinx of a starling. Hannah's singing is echolalic, which means she collects fragments of songs she's heard and weaves them with snippets of others' speech as we interact. Once you acclimate to them, they begin to form a sort of aural tapestry that enlivens the room from behind. For Hannah, however, these songs are not background material; they are foundational to her presence. She calls them her "grounding sounds."

Twenty-seven years old, her chin lifted in a posture of charged engagement, Hannah arranges herself on the couch before preparing to type. Often, just before we get going, she will suddenly get back up and grab a stack of books, desiring their company as she writes. The poets who wrote these books— Emily Dickinson, Gertrude Stein, and Mary Oliver among them—are what Hannah calls "keepers of the light." And it is natural for her to take her place among the keepers because, as they say, she comes by it honestly. Hannah Emerson is verily related to Ralph Waldo Emerson. She is proud of this fact and feels deeply the way it connects her to the legacy of New England light keepers and beyond.

Given my experience with Mark, I should not have been

surprised that the second poem Hannah ever wrote in my presence changed my life. Unlike Mark, Hannah had been immersing herself in poetry for a while before we met, mostly as a listener, though she had recently been trying her hand at writing as well. I make it a point to, as Hannah might put it, expect illumination, but one is never quite prepared for that further step: revelation. During our first meeting, she had written some lines whose rustling resonances took up immediate residence within me: "Some sounds / use words. I hear / the language of leaves." As I reflected on those lines, a chasm opened up between the forceful act of using words and the generous labor of listening to language. Hannah, who doesn't "use words" in the same way I do as a talking person, has learned to orient her body toward the wider and wilder strains of language emanating from all corners of the disparately animate world. As Aviv, Hannah's talented communication partner, helped her adjust the pillows that supported her body, I spoke of the difficulty many people have in leaving the spectacular world long enough to enter that other world, what one might call a listening world, where patience and care and a more capacious form of attention can help us tune in to shier frequencies. I asked Hannah if she would like to write a poem about the listening world. Accepting the resistance of Aviv's hand against her arm, she excitedly typed, "yes" and then "yes" again.

Her poem began, gently, in the imperative:

Say prayer for little
things, things that live
in deep hurt. Feelings
language take to lair.

I was quietly thrilled to see all those trilling *L* words anchoring the lines: little, live, feelings, lair. I was especially taken by the visceral surprise of that final word. While Hannah's first poem, with its "language of leaves," signaled the natural world more directly, this "lair" caused everything before it to grow redolent and feral, crepuscular and furred. And the greater surprise of that animal surge is that it's somehow tied to "language," a marker by which we've often separated ourselves from the animal world. There is a tenderness to the way language is taking these feelings, as if by the hand, into a place where they can be safe and where anything they say can be easily heard, each word amplified by the cave's natural reverberations.

As I took in all of this, Hannah was caught in the echo as well, reverberating in the playful song of her own name: "Haaaaaa-*nuh*, banaaaaaa-*nuh*." Each time she voiced the final syllable it rose precipitously and her hand often dashed into her shirt as if searching for a pendant. More than once she made as if to leave the couch, and Aviv gently welcomed her back, knowing that her abiding desire was to stay with the poem. I pointed out the form I saw emerging, four lines of four words, and asked if that's how Hannah heard and saw the poem. Again she typed, "yes yes," and then "love it." I sensed that this pattern, and the structure it facilitated, was Hannah's way of layering (or even possibly lairing) her own language into place, a mode of angular hospitality to hold and shelter her expression. I asked her how the next stanza would begin, and she was off, her hand occasionally jumping away from Aviv's to open and close the plastic cap of a water bottle:

Let it signal nothing's
light, I say for want
of light feelings. Is my
ear deep or deeper?

Out of the caring darkness of cave lair, the prayer that is
the poem will echo nothing less than the absolute potential of
"nothing's light," a light the poet's feelings momentarily lack,
caught in the heavy reverb of language. But instead of rising
to the surface, like the light that seeks expression at the cave's
mouth, Hannah returns to the question of depth: "Is my / ear
deep or deeper?" I love this question; it may be my favorite to
ever appear in a poem. The poet, as a denizen of the listening
world, has a deep ear, but could it be deeper? Could the poet's
ability to aurally witness, to be present for and with the chorus
of a more-than-human world intensify and grow? This is a ques-
tion the poet Rilke might have asked, or the Buddhist teacher
Pema Chödrön, or one of Hannah's beloved Celtic animists.
It is a question born from years of generative receptivity, ears
attuned to the perching, scurrying, swaying chorus. It is a ques-
tion that instantly reorients the reader toward contemplation,
drawing the spiritual and perceptual into alignment with the
natural.

· · ·

David Abram's journey toward the more-than-human world
began with his curiosity about indigenous shamans. As a
practicing magician, he wanted to know the difference between

magicians and shamans, and he traveled into the heart of several ancient cultures to find an answer. What he discovered is that shamans are people who seek and borrow abilities from the more-than-human world, fundamentally augmenting what human perception and expression entail. They often live on the margin, making their nest in the between. They might be simultaneously less *and* more human than others, depending on what one's definition of human might be. He found that, although they don't always participate in the everyday dialogue of a community, shamans are treasured for their knack at understanding the larger conversation happening around us at all times, a gathering of tongues and colors and unmistakable wit.

Gonzalo Bénard, an autistic artist and shaman, has written about the confluence of shamanic and autistic ways of moving through the world, especially where they meet the neurotypical drive toward bluster: "If you insist or impose verbal communication to an autistic person, you might be unbalancing us, making us more stressed, as we go into silence and humming to find peace and mindfulness so we can recharge and recycle, so we can connect to our higher self and consciousness."[6] Bénard's work points to the oracular within the echolalic, the dervish inside the stim. It's easy to see how Hannah's grounding sounds are no different from Bénard's *om*, giving the contemplative mind a root from which to bloom. It is this mixture of truth, connection, and contemplation that endows autistic thinkers with transformative abilities. They can see what others can't, because their eyes are wide open to the more-than-human world, preferring the periphery to direct contact. They not only hear with greater acuity than their neurotypical counterparts, but also hear more widely, more deeply.

Though it can appear magical, it is not a trick. Autists are listening with care to the chorus already calling out all around us. The strength of their empathy for the more-than-human world gives autistic writers the capacity to completely transform the way we talk about environmental crisis. I believe autistic wisdom can play a necessary part in facing this pandemic, or climate change, or whatever new immune response arises from a planet combating the humanmade Anthropocene. We, as a species, need to enter a stage of deep listening if we are to survive. Our listening must grow, as Hannah wrote, ever deeper.

. . .

Despite her echolalic grounding sounds, Hannah does not find it possible to produce consistent spoken language of her own accord. She can sing and repeat, can even compose by song on rare occasion, but she cannot physiologically organize her poetic voice into speech on a consistent basis. Many months after writing this poem, when I asked Hannah whether she felt a sense of purpose in her engagement with the listening world, she responded, "Yes, try to understand. I am not really human. I am helpful mistake of humanity."

Hannah is one of the most human and humane people I know, but she lives in a society where her manner of moving through the world cannot find a fluid way with our contemporary expectations and mores. She is seen by some as less-than-human, a terrible paradox given her rich engagement with the more-than-human world. This is a paradox explored with great care by Sunaura Taylor in her book *Beasts of Burden: Animal and Disability Liberation.* In tracing how ratios of human and animal are projected onto disabled (and raced) individuals, Taylor also attempts to hold open the possibility that embracing the animal parts of who we are might allow us to live in a more ethical, perhaps natural manner. But "the natural," as Taylor reminds us, is tricky territory: "The reality [is] that we can never see nature through lenses that are not our own; we can never separate something called 'nature' from our human perceptions of it."[7]

And yet, I'm curious about the way neurodivergent perceptions of the world might actually exceed the "human" lens. If Hannah, as she writes, is "not really human," perhaps it's because her engagement with nature is so intensely more-than-human. In the many months since she wrote "The Listening World," Hannah has returned over and over to the intrinsic communicability she finds in nature, detailing what she gleans from majestic hummingbirds to mushrooms to the oft-shunned housefly. Hannah does not seem to feel set apart from nature by her perceptions, but very much enmeshed through them. As you read the following poems, each touching another seam where the animal and human are woven together, I want you to return to Hannah's question. She doesn't ask whether her ear is deep, but whether it is deeper. Hannah is ready to face this question, to live into it, but as a society, as a species, are we?

Animal Ear

I hear great trying free sounds that you
do not hear yes it is

hard to try to live trying to hear the way
I do and you go listen

to me really hard to hear both at the same
time. I hear the vibrations

of your thoughts. I hear helpful plants
grow to the sun. I hear

the sun rays of healing light becoming
life freedom to breathe

life into hopeful hopeful life. I hear
the vibrations of fear

coming from everyone holding fear
in their mussy lives

of nothing life. I hear you trying to help
me great teachers

of the normal way of hearing. Please
learn from me because

it is hard being meet me great humans
just try greet me with fullness

of your lovely soul. When you turn
your thoughts to find reality of hearing

you will find me and your free animal
trying to hear helpful messages for you

from the animal trying to bite you.

And then another:

Between

Love the noun her trying
to be the noun that is
me keep trying but I feel
more like an it. Please
really feel like me is it.

Love being me beautiful
life makes me feel like
an it. Please stop seeing
me keep noticing being
the great moments I am

not an it. It great great
it it it it. It flows between
nonhuman animal tree

look to all the it it around
me they are great beings

that have been labeled
it too. Lovely tree lovely
rock lovely stream lovely
animal great mountain
we are all it because you

great spirit of great life
forget how to really are.
Please stop thinking
of yourself as an it.
It it beautiful it.

And another:

Becoming Mud

Please be with me great free animals. I want to be
with you great being of light. Please see me great

nobody nobody nobody hell animals trying to go
to helpful keepers of the knowledge try to go

to the place in the mud that is where I try to live
in peace great mud of this great kissing loving

earth lovely messy yucky in mud on my face if
kissing mother loving me is the great animal

that is named Hannah. Please greet me in
the mud it is great mess please go to oh

the bucket to get the water to try to make
more mud yes. Please try to get the mud

helpful to you if you become mud too.
Please get that great animals are all

autistic. Please love poets we are the first
autistics. Love this secret no one knows it.

There are so many insights to be gleaned, to be *felt*, in these poems, that it's difficult to know where to begin. You can imagine the joy I experience seeing Hannah claim her connection to the first poets (and animals). This is part of her legacy as a keeper of the light. All that the neurotypical world views as base, animalistic, subhuman, Hannah recuperates through her wisdom and generosity. In the mud, she finds the root of light. In the mundane, she finds an undaunted faith. In the troubling nounness of being an imperiled being, she finds a pathway to presence. Her way in the world teems with abundance, permeated with the beautiful it-ness of ecological systems. This is what Erin Manning and Brian Massumi call "the dance of attention," a mode of neurodiverse engagement that is characterized not by "attentiveness of the human *to* the environment but attentiveness *of* the environment to its own flowering."[8] Instead of responding *to* nature, autists are often keenly aware of how they *are* nature. And the poetry they write isn't simply *about* nature but verily participates in the broad expressivity of the natural world.

Hannah's poetry emerges, letter by letter, word by word, from its steadily tilled soil like a spontaneous garden, nourishing the reader with its gifts. I often find myself overwhelmed by the simultaneously wild and cultivated vibrancy of her poems—like a sudden spring day here in Minneapolis after the long white winter. I could easily write ten pages about each of Hannah's poems, but perhaps in encountering them this way, insight upon insight, you can apprehend some of the nearly relentless creativity she brings to our sessions each week. Creativity and *generosity*. Every day I work with Hannah is a tremendous gift. In the epilogue to *Braiding Sweetgrass*, Potawatomi ecologist Robin Wall Kimmerer, who literally (literarily?) lives just down the road from Hannah, writes: "Generosity is simultaneously a moral and material imperative, especially among people who live close to the land and know its waves of plenty and scarcity. Where the well-being of one is linked to the well-being of all."[9]

In the seemingly endless waves of scarcity brought on by late-stage capitalism, you can often find "the animal trying to bite you" with its urgent warning, but it is also trying to bite you back toward abundance. Only then can we discover the waves of plenty that await us, a true and deep well-being that can only arise from what Kimmerer terms "mutual flourishing." What better way to describe the rich promise of the neurodiversity movement?

Our bodies each possess a generous proclivity, a well-being that is linked to the well-being of our families, our neighbors, our co-workers, our strangers, and the vast tangle of more-than-human voices all crying out in the song of survival. We need a chorus. And we need to ensure that this chorus can encompass every possible note, every possible phrasing, every possible rhythm and intensity. One of those notes will be Hannah's, and she wants you to know that her singing is both difficult and necessary. During a recent session, she offered up her own definition of autism: "It is very hard to be awake in this world. My body makes it hard to be here with you. Please understand you helpful people put the label on my existence. Please get this hell is mine. It is great life of trying to be here, because I help the world get that they need to become me to help themselves." The mutual flourishing of our neurodiverse future will require singing and listening in equal measure, our ears and throats (and hearts) growing ever deeper as we transform these disconnected songs of survival into a thriving, wild chorus.

A Brand New Outfit

Thirteen Ways of Looking at Dwight D. Eisenhower—Blasts
Off Past the Stars—Hot Dogs and Snowflakes—He Would
Be a Downpour—Paradoxes Abound—The Alapa Body—
Transformation Transformed—Everything Will Change—
Daqwhan Makes a Cocoon of Daqwhan

I had just finished my first writing session with a different Max,
with no relation to the Eati family, or was about to, when he
stood up and declared in a firm voice, "Next week I want to
write about Dwight D. Eisenhower." Given that we'd spent our
last hour writing poems about hockey and Claymation sheep, I
was momentarily stunned by his announcement. "Absolutely," I
said after I'd gathered myself. "I'll write his name down on the
next page, just so we remember."

When Max, at once intense and friendly, arrived the fol-
lowing Monday, he made a beeline for the seat next to me
and said, "I'm ready to write about Dwight D. Eisenhower."
I asked whether he knew much about the former president. "I
know that he was president from 1953 to 1961," Max replied,
"and I know he played hockey." I said that was a fine start.
Opening up my laptop, I suggested we get to know Ike a little
better before Max started to write his poem. We scoured several

websites, cherry-picking facts here and there. Ike, like any human being, was quite interesting when you gave him a good look. I could tell Max was starting to get antsy, so I shifted to a discussion of form.

"Can I show you a poem?" I asked him. He nodded. I opened up Wallace Stevens's classic poem "Thirteen Ways of Looking at a Blackbird." We read through the poem once and I answered Max's questions about the vocabulary: pantomime, innuendo, euphony, equipage. He liked how each section of the poem offered its own perspective on the blackbird. The ideas, though difficult to grasp, seemed to excite him. In preparing to write, he took off his shoes, much like a character in a film takes off his shirt when preparing to fight, but Max did it carefully, intentionally, as if seeking to open up more of himself to the air.

The poem began in a plainly factual vein:

Thirteen Ways of Looking at Dwight D. Eisenhower

1.
He was an active boy.
He played hockey.

2.
He was president from 1953 to 1961.
He was a great president.

Here I stopped Max to ask if we might follow Stevens's lead, reaching beyond the plainness of "great" to something more vibrant. Max smiled wide and said "deluxe."

In the third section Max stated that Ike was liked. I asked Max why Ike was liked. He thought about it for a moment and his eyes brightened, as he seemed to catch something unexpected: "I think people liked him because of his smile. And also he made the interstates." Despite the present-day debate around automobile use and carbon footprints, I agreed that these two things were eminently likeable. Section four covered his military career. Section five focused on his establishment of the National Aeronautics and Space Administration: "He created / the NASA space company / that goes up into space." I wondered aloud if that final line of section five might not desire some rewording. I pointed out the grammatical nuance, but also the flatness of the phrase "goes up into space." Max erased the line, thought for a moment, and then wrote, "that blasts off past the stars." I told him how much I admired the assonance of his new line, how "that," "blasts," and "past" all deftly echoed the central syllabic sound of "NASA."

For the past few sections I'd noticed Max's eyes moving toward the far window of the room. Our session, supported by the Autism Society of Minnesota, was located on the top floor of the Open Book, a literary arts building in downtown Minneapolis, in a room generously gifted to us by The Loft Literary Center. Outside, the clouds were accumulating, darkening. Even the light in the room was changing, growing dim and ominous. I attempted to refocus Max on the poem, where he had just suggested Ike might like tasty foods: "What kinds of tasty foods?" Without turning from the window he replied dreamily, "Hot dogs and snowflakes." This is where it becomes clear, to paraphrase Frank O'Hara, why I am not a history teacher. I added Max's answer and watched him stare deeper into the gathering storm.

I asked Max if he had any corrections to the line, but he answered with a question of his own, "Can we write a weather poem?" He was now standing to get a better view of the black-green sky. I told him I would love to write a weather poem—that, in fact, I had written a whole book of poems called *Becoming Weather*. Max lifted one of his eyebrows. But . . . I also felt strongly that Dwight D. Eisenhower deserved to know his final four ways. I could tell that Max wanted to please me, wanted to finish the poem, but that he also couldn't tear himself away from the storm, which I had to admit was now a churning spectacle of monstrous proportions. Finally, he turned to me and said, firmly, "I *have* to write a weather poem." I could see there was no hope for Ike. Just as I was about to relent, my eyes returned to section nine. I had an idea. "Max, do you think it might be possible to combine our Dwight D. Eisenhower poem with a poem about weather? Section nine already set the precedent."

Max immediately sat back down. "How?" he said simply. I thought for a moment and then asked if it would be possible to reverse-personify Ike, to choose a kind of weather to represent him. Max moved the laptop in front of him and typed, "I think he would be a rain cloud." I asked him what Ike's voice sounded like. He smiled and typed, "Loud like thunder." I asked him whether Ike resembled any other kind of weather. He looked at his earlier answer and then typed and said simultaneously, "I think he would be a looming rain cloud." I told him how much I admired the specificity of "looming." Then his smile and eyes both widened. He pressed return and typed, "I think he would be a downpour." He read the line out loud with delicious emphasis, his voice rising on "downpour" into an ecstatic squeal.

Thirteen Ways of Looking at Dwight D. Eisenhower

1.
He was an active boy.
He played hockey.

2.
He was president from 1953 to 1961.
He was a deluxe president.

3.
People liked him
because they enjoyed his smile.
He came up with the idea
of interstates.

4.
He was a veteran
of the Second World War.
I think he did a good job
serving as commander.

5.
He created
the NASA space company
that blasts off past the stars.

6.
He retired in 1961.
He lived in Gettysburg.

7.
I think he was attentive
and thought a lot
about people's feelings.

8.
He cherished opera
because the singing is charming.

9.
I think Ike liked tasty foods
like hot dogs and snowflakes.

10.
I think he would be a rain cloud.

11.
Loud like thunder.

12.
I think he would be a looming rain cloud.

13.
I think he would be a downpour.

. . .

There is more than one paradox at the heart of autism. Or, as M. Remi Yergeau writes, "When it comes to stories of autism, paradoxes abound."[1] The primary paradox, of course, is that autists may seem to be "in a world of their own," when they are often paying far greater attention to the fullness of the world around them than anyone else in the room. There is also the way autistic students habitually skew toward the literal, despite possessing undeniable gifts for figurative thought. Then there are the nonspeaking autists, like Hannah and Adam, who, despite being physically unable to produce audible verse, are some of the most lyrical writers I've known, autistic or otherwise. But what I'm thinking about now is the autistic struggle for what researchers call "cognitive flexibility," or the capacity to incorporate change, which is coupled, in so many of my students, with a fascination for transition and hybridity, a thrall for metamorphosis and transformation. Think of Brian's cryptozoological curiosity, or Hannah's animal it, or this poem co-written by Mark and Max Eati, which deftly echoes Sid's "Volcanic Mind":

A Volcano Named Eati

A volcano named Eati
erupts inside our bellies
at the sound of a pattern
family member's pattern of joy
or pattern of worry

We experience synchronous
and asynchronous changes
good and bad
heavy and light

We laugh like
the alapa pattern
starting at our heads and
ending at our toes

We scream when it
rocks our bellies
like the pattern of a song
pattern of drumming
alapa pattern of emotional pain

We feel the
joy and pain
in our alapa bodies
all over our navels
all over almost everything

An alapa is the underlying rhythmic beat of an Indian raga, which is a musical form characterized by its lively and syncopated repetition. Ragas, like many musical and poetic forms, are deeply invested in patterns and moments that deviate from them. I adore the way Mark and Max reinvent the autistic body as the alapa body, a porous mode of being suffused with musical patterns and intensities. The changes they feel, in their sibling closeness, come to resemble a volcano erupting with both joy and pain. Change can be difficult and welcome at the same time, forcing us into unexpected transformations.

Our other Max is fascinated by weather because of the way it changes, especially on a summer day in the Midwest like the one we spent writing about Dwight D. Eisenhower. His fascination forced us to transform Ike into a rainstorm. And perhaps that's one of the most frightening things about transformation: change begets change.

It is widely claimed that autistic individuals struggle with executive function—the ability to organize one's thoughts and actions and emotions to suit the business of life—and professionals often zero in on flexibility as a unique challenge. While new research is complicating this idea, I've seen the most soft-spoken and gentle student lash out with real violence when the changes in their schedule are too much for them to bear.[2] But what if this outcry is heard as a desire to belong and succeed? As Barry Prizant points out in his book *Uniquely Human*, this desire is where our most nuanced attention should be paid: "Some professionals work hard to seize control from children with autism, but when they do, they're not helping; they're causing increased dysregulation by interfering with the children's strategy to stay well-regulated."[3]

By introducing the topic of transformation into my work with students, I am partially attempting to restore some modicum of efficacy. I am giving them a delineated space where they can write their way into a certain creative dominion over change. As writers, they can explore anxiety-causing ideas within a framework that allows them to process the mechanisms and implications of those ideas without becoming overwhelmed. And, more than not, students will eventually reveal a fascination with transformation, whether it has to do with werewolves, butter-flies, or extreme home makeovers.

Students' curiosity about transformation may also signal an understanding of how they are perceived by the larger world. Brian is not my only student pulled toward the mysterious corners of cryptozoology. Where it concerns creatures like the various ape-men—why never an ape-woman?—the concept of something simultaneously human and not-human can be a source of deep and sustained inquiry. It resonates with the way my students too often find themselves relegated to a not-quite-human status by a world that seeks to examine and explain them, more than not as a sort of subhuman or extra-human freak that allows neurotypical society to appreciate by contrast how very "normal" it is.

My students, for whom change can be frightening, none-theless seem to thrive when facing change head-on in their po-ems. It's as if their poetic imagination works as a leavening force against the oppressive and often arbitrary pressure they face every day, a pressure that asks them to move in accordance with the whims and demands of others. For students so regularly asked to change themselves to suit "normal" expectations, change can feel exhausting and invasive. Within the relatively safe, circum-scribed, and playful field of the poem, transformation can be a territory that is explored, lightened, and, somehow, transformed itself.

When I first delved directly into this territory with Wal-lace, a bright and exuberant young man with a penchant for color, it was our last writing session before the winter holidays. Snow had settled over the roofs in Minneapolis and was falling in great fresh piles where Wallace lived as well. Knowing Wallace had an affinity for the concept of metamorphosis— the word itself felt like a sort of talisman for him—I suggested that the snow was reminiscent of a cocoon, softly wrapping itself around both our worlds. He liked this image very much, and, sensing his enthusiasm, I wondered aloud what cocoons the other seasons might make. Wallace understood this challenge immediately and he leapt into writing a poem around the theme of cocoons and metamorphosis.

In Wallace's poem, change is made familiar. His various cocoons are not frightening at all; they protect and insulate as the effects of metamorphosis take place: snow, flowers, sun, leaves. In the poem, the world defends and adorns itself simultaneously: bright white, parti-colored petals, yellow-gold, falling finally in soft orange and rich red. But Wallace reminds us that everything will change yet again in the new year. No matter how much we attempt to brace against change, in fact, no matter how much we attempt to embrace change, it will always feel a little like being pried from our own skin, even if that means emerging with something like wings.

The leaves, the clothes, the stories: these are all cocoons we forge against the tide of new seats and new calendars. Wallace's poem itself is a story, or even the rehearsal of a story, made more powerful by its metaphors and music. I hope writing it brought Wallace a little closer to his own powers of protection, the folded wings of his imagination forming a snug, vibrant buffer against the days to come.

. . .

In Minnesota we have the same four seasons as everyone else, they just occur with different proportions. The Dakota, who have known Minnesota (or Mni Sóta) the longest, break down the year as follows: five months of winter, followed by one month of spring, followed by five months of summer, followed by one month of fall.[4] I often teach twin residencies at the South Education Center in the fall and spring, and inevitably the students are drawn toward poems that chronicle or reflect Minnesota's rapidly transforming landscape, which reaches a nearly untenable acceleration during the months of October and April. The world is suddenly beyond recognition, sometimes overnight. It reminds me of another passage from Dara McAnulty's *Diary of a Young Naturalist*: "All week I've been like this, intensely excited, nervous, for reasons I may never truly understand. Perhaps it's because I love new places and hate new places all at once. The smells, the sounds. Things that nobody else notices."[5] Though Dara is literally writing of new places, he is writing about them at the turn of spring, and I think spring's ability to turn entire landscapes into new places cannot be overstated. The smells, the sounds: when you have an autistic gift for sensory perception, these moments of transformation can feel exhilarating and overwhelming and alienating and a thousand other things simultaneously, a new and garish world bubbling up from under the neutral blanket of winter.

Something special happens when I bring a poem from one of my students into a new classroom. Eyes perk up, heads subconsciously calculating how long it will take for the poem they write to travel into further classrooms, obtaining a brand of academic notoriety. When I entered Stephanie Hawley's classroom and announced my writing idea for that day, she thanked me for finding a way to dovetail with the science curriculum. I was confused. She informed me that the class had been studying metamorphosis! After I shared Wallace's poem, Zach, Stephanie's most outspoken student (a different Zach from the one featured in Chapter 3), chimed in, "Yeah, that poem is wrong." I raised my eyebrows. "Butterflies make a chrysalis, not a cocoon," he continued. "Only moths make cocoons." Blushing a little at my ignorance, I thanked Zach for filling me in.

Stephanie's students, younger autists with a contagious (if sometimes raucous) energy, are usually up for any idea I have, and they often take poems in unexpected directions. Zach and three of his classmates—Dylan, Tarin, and Daqwhan—took turns trying the form out:

Winter makes a chrysalis
Of snow as it turns into spring

Spring makes a chrysalis
Of butterflies as it turns into summer

Summer makes a cocoon
Of flowers as it turns into fall

Fall makes a cocoon
Of scary costumes as it turns into winter

I love the meta-metamorphosis of spring, as it forges its chrysalis from countless chrysalis-forming insects. And while winter and summer were somewhat predictable, fall also offered a novel take on transformation. It was late October and we were nearing Halloween. The special night of sanctioned if temporary metamorphosis was on everyone's minds. Each student returned to the poem, imagining a cocoon or chrysalis uniquely tailored to help him make his idiosyncratic transformation.

Zach was first and announced that he wanted to transform into an airplane. When I asked him how he would accomplish this miraculous metamorphosis, he looked at me with a piteous expression and said, "Dreams!" When I asked him what dreams are made of, he gave me the same disappointed look, as if I were asking the most sophomoric questions possible, and said, "Sleep!" So Zach's cocoon of sleep would help him dream his way into airplane mode.

Next was Dylan, quiet counterpoint to Zach's boisterous swagger. Dylan spent all our sessions together assiduously drawing with thick-tipped markers on cut pieces of recycled paper. Often, at the completion of a poem, he would hand me a drawing to keep. I asked Dylan whether he wanted a chrysalis or a cocoon. After repeating the question a couple of times, he chose chrysalis. When I asked him what he would like to transform into, he stopped drawing for a short moment and said, "Caterpillar." I smiled at the reversal. When I was halfway through asking him what kind of chrysalis he would need, Dylan suddenly blurted out, "Wiggles!" I told him how much I admired the assonance of those short *I* sounds: chrysalis, wiggles, caterpillar. And so Dylan's chrysalis of wiggles would let him reverse his way from butterfly to caterpillar.

Next was Tarin, who very rarely uttered even a single word during our sessions but was usually bent over his small whiteboard with a dry-erase marker. Instead of relying on Tarin to tell us the answers, we could often refer directly to his board, on which he was always carefully writing meticulous block-letter script. When I asked Tarin what he might want to become, he was laboriously forming the letters of a prospective movie title: "Mr. Incredible 2." I asked if it would be okay to use that for the poem. He nodded in assent. Then I asked him what kind of cocoon he would need to make the transformation. He didn't respond. Tarin's aide, Maria, repeated the question a few times before giving him some choices. When she offered "muscles," he broke his silent concentration to repeat the word, "Muscles." And so Tarin's cocoon of muscles would seamlessly morph him into Mr. Incredible 2.

Finally, it was Daqwhan's turn. Daqwhan was feeling dys-regulated by something, possibly the content of the poem we were writing. He was mumbling insults toward Zach under his breath and giving him a sidelong glare. Stephanie asked Daqwhan if he needed his putty, and he nodded his head. Putty in hand, kneading the dark blue blob into shape, he seemed to gather himself. I asked him whether he would make a chrysalis or a cocoon. "Cocoon," he said shortly. I asked him what the cocoon would be made of, and after repeating the question a few times he answered, "Daqwhan." I told him how much I liked the idea that we could make a cocoon of ourselves. It was an act of self-sufficiency or even *self-reliance*, as Ralph Waldo would have it. When I asked what transformation this cocoon of himself would occasion, he said, "I would turn into a werewolf."

Our poem was nearly complete. As I was about to ask the class what we should title our poem, Dylan handed me the piece of paper on which he'd been drawing. On the left side of the page was a yellow caterpillar and on the right side was an orange butterfly. At the top of the page a sign hung down, emblazoned with the words "A Brand New Outfit." And so it was. I added the title and we read the poem aloud, amid lots of laughter:

A Brand New Outfit

Winter makes a chrysalis
Of snow as it turns into spring

Spring makes a chrysalis
Of butterflies as it turns into summer

Summer makes a cocoon
Of flowers as it turns into fall

Fall makes a cocoon
Of scary costumes as it turns into winter

Zach makes a cocoon of sleep
As he turns into an airplane

Dylan makes a chrysalis of wiggles
As he turns into a caterpillar

Tarin makes a cocoon of muscle
As he turns into Mr. Incredible 2

Daqwhan makes a cocoon of Daqwhan
As he turns into a werewolf

I Can Be My Real Self

Ballast and Buoy—A Great Deal About Gender—Magical
Memories—A Dreamer Who Dreams—A Pattern in the
World

Think about the person whose presence—real or imagined—
makes you feel calm, the person who makes you feel the
most contentedly *you*. Or maybe it's not a person, but a piece of
clothing. Or maybe it's a place. For teenage Wallace, whom you
met in the last chapter, it can be all of these things, but primar-
ily it's the actress Courteney Cox. When Wallace thinks about
Courteney, the world's variegated chaos recedes and is replaced
with a surge of inner warmth, suffused with sweetness and cour-
age.[1] The challenges of being autistic sometimes provoke a dire
need to quell the world's cacophonous din. And so, despite its
implausibility, Wallace's reliance on Courteney Cox has become a
ballast and buoy when the storms of life inevitably arise. At times,
his reliance turns into something more. There are even moments
when Wallace *becomes* Courteney. It's a magical transformation
that allows him to discover what he calls his "true self."

The best word to describe Wallace is "ebullient." He has an
eager, magical smile that buzzes like a neon sign atop his lanky
frame. He is not shy. In fact, his readiness to engage belies many

presumed characteristics of autism. If a Farrelly brothers' film is referenced, Wallace nearly explodes thinking aloud about the funniest scenes, asks repeatedly whether you remember them, but sometimes doesn't stop long enough to hear your answer. He always leads with words (I've never seen him without some form of language emblazoned on his shirt) and is ready to discuss anything, though one may find even the most erudite of topics eventually bends back toward bathroom humor.

When I first met Wallace, it was at a program he'd been attending for several years. When I asked if he'd like to write a poem, he replied, "I think that would be great!" Then I asked him what his favorite thing in the world was. He answered, "Bikinis!" "Any particular color?" I inquired. Wallace: "Purple!" His exclamatory style makes his eclectic range of interests seem almost self-evident. You start thinking to yourself, "Bikinis *are* great." He quickly embarked on a remarkable journey that became a poem with each line featuring a different woman in a different purple bikini in a different location, each time leaning as far into specificity as possible. Wallace had no trouble articulating visually striking lines, even while many people, including his father and his longtime occupational therapist, observed. Sometimes a crowd can inhibit a student's ability to perform and sometimes it can actually enhance it. Until I know a student very well, I'm never sure which effect observation will have, so I generally like to keep things intimate. But it seemed to be working for Wallace.

About three-quarters of the way through the composition of his poem, I asked Wallace who the next woman would be. He answered with a question, "Does it have to be a woman?" Intrigued, I said it most certainly did not. Then he asked another question, a little sheepishly, "Can it be . . . *me*?" I watched his father's eyes widen, surprised but warmly supportive. Even his occupational therapist was caught off guard by the revelation. Wallace then went on to describe how he sometimes ventures down into his basement and puts on a bikini, which makes him feel calm. And so it was that the bright surfaces of Wallace's poem, so reminiscent of mail-order catalogue descriptions, took on an unexpected depth.

Wallace's revelation may have been surprising to us in the moment, but he's far from alone in his desire to experience and explore gender beyond binary lines. Gender nonconformity is actually seven times more common among Wallace's autistic peers than among the general population.[2] Many potential causes have been suggested for this overlap. Some researchers hypothesize that it has a biological component, while others see it as an outgrowth of the way autists process social literacy, while still others see it as evidence of gender as a restricted fixation. In my experience, "cause" and "autism" almost never come together in a satisfying or even meaningful way, but the implications of this statistic are worth discussion. Perhaps, as many autistic writers have done before, we could shift from thinking of a cause to thinking about a series of practices or resistances, widely embodied by the term "neuroqueer."[3] As Nick Walker has written, it's a word that is not limited to gender or sexuality but seeks to open up possibilities where others are pinning them down, drawing attention to how autistic lives often diverge from multiple forms of normativity simultaneously.[4] As someone who thinks a great deal about gender, I find this autistic propensity for nonbinary ways of moving through the world to be very exciting. I love the idea that autistic individuals might escape or eschew some forms of social conditioning that limit and enforce the possibilities of self-identification, leaving them freer to form gender identities that complicate or exceed whatever binaries are placed before them.

That being said, an autist who also identifies as gender variant must navigate social complexity on a whole other level. The tendency among autists to miss or ignore social cues both insulates them from normative gender conditioning and renders them doubly at risk to its social enforcement. When Wallace revels in the scatology of *Dumb and Dumber*, his interests align with the expectations of a young man his age, but even he realizes that donning a bikini is something he might be wary to share outside the poem's safe haven. We live in a world where a young man who loves bathroom humor could find dire legal consequences for his choice of bathroom.

Some weeks later, Wallace expressed a desire to write about Courteney Cox, reveling aloud in the alliteration of her name. He chose to write a poem that utilized alliteration in every line, the poem crackling with sound. Wallace expressed how holding Courteney in his thoughts, much like the snug pressure of the bikini, made Wallace feel calm and happy. In the final lines of the poem, Courteney puts an arm around him, and they share magical memories about childhood.

In yet another poem, Wallace wrote about the way his "self" transforms to meet different stages of his day, revealing multiple aspects of who his is and can be. At the end of that poem, Wallace lets himself imagine transforming into Courteney and that helps him sleep. The final lines describe a boy that is finally asleep in bed, a dreamer who dreams. And in a delicious bit of repetition, this dreamer dreams about Courteney. This, Wallace contends, is a place where he can be his real self, a boy who loves alliteration and dreams of people who make him feel calm, people among whom he feels an unfettered belonging.

All of us, autistic and otherwise, move through our days adopting different personae to fit different situations. This strategic metamorphosis is a crucial aspect of how we negotiate the social world. For an autist this shifting performance of self has higher stakes, as it constitutes the core of a perceived social deficit—a deficit aggressively targeted by applied behavioral analysis–style therapies. And recent articles have questioned whether ABA therapy, in coaching autistic individuals to act less autistic, also encourages them to hide their real selves.[5] Behavioral models, after all, are intrinsically designed to alter behavior. And while there are self-injurious "behaviors" (which Prizant and others would stress are fundamentally communications) that require immediate attention, much of what constitutes "behavior" is the desire to find pattern in the world, a series of patterns that perform a self.

If we add the further layer of gender, which society conditions from a surprisingly young age, one begins to appreciate the immense pressure young men like Wallace feel to perform a variety of selves designed, not to express themselves, but to please others. Or worse, to keep the people around them comfortable. Or even worse, to act in complicity with a world that wants us to collaboratively enforce misogynist and heteronormative modes of being. The wonderful irony is that autists may be defying gender binaries precisely because they don't affirm what society is trying to teach them. Many autists I know, and many neurodivergent people more broadly, are demanding a neuroqueer redefinition of gender that can help us all move past destructive cultural norms.[6]

All young men like Wallace deserve a venue where they can discover and express their true selves. *Everyone* deserves a forum where they can discover and express their most authentic selves. Perhaps Wallace's connection with Courteney Cox can help others find language to celebrate and articulate who they are when no one's asking them to be someone else. Autistic voices are cultivating spaces where we can all ask more nuanced questions about gender, questions that our patriarchal and often punitive culture tends to drown out. We are beginning, finally, to understand that there is no "normal" brain. Can the lessons of neurodiversity push us to escape the rigid binaries of gender as well?

Becoming Rainbow Man

Feeling Rich—To Hide for Prey—She Watches Over Me—
Rainbow Man Is a Wrestler—Full of Dark Pink—Inviting
Darkness—The Best Party Ever

Lonnie begins most of our sessions by insisting that he will
not be writing today. I've learned to hang back and wait
for him to initiate our writing himself. Today I was talking
about the strange ovoid water tower visible from the park-
ing lot of the South Education Center, scholastic home to so
many of my students: Mark, Daqwhan, Dylan, Khalil, and
Lonnie among them. The water tower, which is perched atop
seven spindly cylindrical legs, resembles some sort of giant
squid or alien vessel. It reads RICHFIELD in thick white
letters cut out from a blue background. I was telling Lon-
nie's aide, Tommy, how it made me think about richness, and
since Tommy used to play basketball professionally, I used
a hoops metaphor: "I don't have all that much money, but
when I shoot a three-pointer and it quietly swishes through
the net . . . I feel *rich*."

I said this loud enough for Lonnie to overhear, and it immediately got his attention. Lonnie, as he wrote in the bio of his first chapbook of poems, "grew up poor." He's just about to turn eighteen and has been living in different group homes for several years now. He thinks a lot about the money he'd like to have or will one day earn. After publishing several chapbooks and receiving some modest royalties, he even sees poetry as a possible means to self-sufficiency. His poetry has given him a voice in places, like school board meetings and trans equity summits, where he's beginning to feel a sense of power and belonging. "What are y'all talking about?" he asks, sidling up to my open laptop, which has the words "Feeling Rich" written as an invitation at the top of the page. "Feeling Rich, huh? What you mean by feeling rich?" I gave him another example. "When I put on a new pair of yellow sunglasses, even if they only cost me five dollars, I feel *rich*. What makes you feel rich, Lonnie?"

And off he went. I could tell from his initial momentum that Lonnie was ready to write an epic one. So I suggested he write an abecedarian poem, working his way through each letter of the alphabet, for a total of twenty-six lines. Lonnie was game. Occasionally, I'd pause to ask him a question, trying to draw out greater specificity. When Lonnie said eating an orange makes him feel rich, I asked him where he would eat it: "In the jungle." When Lonnie said working with sick animals makes him feel rich, I asked him what kind of animals: "Cheetahs." When he said zebras make him feel rich, I asked him what he would do with a zebra: "Ride it." I asked him where: "Through the woods." I asked him when: "In the middle of the night."

Feeling Rich

A warm Alabama vacation makes me feel rich
Batman makes me feel rich
Chocolate chip pancakes with bacon and eggs and sausage
    and hash browns and orange juice make me feel rich
Buying some Nike shorts and a shirt from Dick's Sporting
    Goods makes me feel rich
Adorable baby elephants make me feel rich
Watching Teddy Bridgewater get tackled by the Green Bay
    Packers makes me feel rich
Buying NBA Live 2018 at Gamestop makes me feel rich
Getting a hug from Aaron Rodgers makes me feel rich
Sleeping in an igloo makes me feel rich
Strawberry jelly and butter on my biscuits makes me feel rich
Being King of the World makes me feel rich
A lion's roar makes me feel rich
Getting hyper drinking Mountain Dew makes me feel rich
Spending a nickel makes me feel rich
Eating an orange in the jungle makes me feel rich
Plums make me feel rich
Not quitting makes me feel rich
Seeing a big rat makes me feel rich
Sleeping all day makes me feel rich
When I feel like a tiny tiger I feel rich
Using an umbrella in the rain makes me feel rich
Working with sick cheetahs makes me feel rich
Riding an extra big roller coaster makes me feel rich
Why you leave me when I'm feeling rich?

> Riding a zebra in the woods in the middle of the night makes
> me feel rich

This was the last poem I helped Lonnie write during the 2017–2018 school year. Lonnie identifies with male pronouns, so that's what I use to describe him, even when I'm chronicling moments that occurred before he embraced his current identity. When we first met earlier that fall, the name on my schedule said "Lonnae," and Lonnie publicly identified with female pronouns. At the end of the year, Lonnie edited the final versions of his poems to reflect male pronouns throughout, but the original drafts of his poems record the story of a sudden transformation, at least in its public iteration, and I will let those drafts speak for themselves.

On the first day I was led into his classroom, Lonnie shyly let himself be coaxed over to a small table so we could write. He spoke in a soft, tenor voice, helping to communicate his initial timidity. I started, as I often do with students I'm meeting for the first time, by asking Lonnie what he loved to think about. I would later find out he loved to think about all kinds of things, especially transformation and the quarterback Aaron Rodgers, but on this day he looked at me blankly and then shook his head.

I told him it was okay if he couldn't think of anything right now and added, "The thing I really love to think about is words." I asked him if he had heard about alliteration. He hadn't. I explained how alliteration involved putting several words together in a sentence to create a pleasing, repetitive sound and then gave an example off the top of my head: "Chris can't keep from clapping his claws." Lonnie smiled. I asked him if he knew of any animals whose names started with *L*. He smiled again and said, "Lion." I asked him what he loved about lions, and he answered alliteratively, "Loud roars." I asked him if he could write "Lonnae loves loud lion roars," and he began methodically constructing the words, letter by letter, on the lined paper in front of him, sounding them out as he went, frequently asking for help. Lonnie is a neurodivergent learner, the type of student the South Education Center is designed to serve. He has a range of challenges, both cognitive and social, which complement his range of strengths, anchored by his rich imagination. When Lonnie was done, I asked him to read the line and he said, "Lonnie loves loud lion roars." I looked more closely at the page and saw that it indeed read "Lonnie." "Would you like me to call you Lonnie?" I asked. He nodded.

Thinking we might continue the alliteration game, I asked if Lonnie was fond of any other animals. "Octopus," he said without hesitation. I smiled and admitted that the octopus was a favorite of mine as well. I asked him what he loved about the octopus. "Octopus blends in," he said. I asked him why. "To hide for prey." I asked him what else an octopus does. "Octopus turns red to scare other animals." The alliteration, having jump-started the process, was now falling away like a spent booster rocket.

I asked Lonnie if he ever liked to hide like the octopus. He nodded his head. "Where?" I asked. Suddenly his voice changed, growing deeper and more confident: "People always act like I'm mad or something. They don't like my face." I asked him what it was that people didn't like about his face.

He angled his chin down and looked at me with a mixture of irritation and pity: "They don't like that it's so *black*." I asked him how it made him feel when people misrepresented him and assumed he was mad or threatening. "When they stare?" he asked. I nodded. Lonnie's voice changed again, jumping an octave: "It makes me surprised." This alteration made me think about the hiding "for" and wonder whether it wasn't also hiding "from."

The springboard of these questions helped Lonnie write the last two stanzas of the poem much more quickly than the first. I asked him what he wanted to call it and he said, proudly, "All About Me."

All About Me

Lonnie loves loud lion roars
Octopus blends in and hides for prey
Octopus turns red to scare other animals

Lonnie blends into a black wall
Other people become scared of Lonnie
Because they think her face looks mad and upset

When octopus get surprised
They ink a blackish purple everywhere
Lonnie gets surprised when people stare

The ending, which I love, immediately reminded me of the end of another poem: "Blanch-Ink-Jet Maneuver," written by

DJ Savarese about the work of autist Stephen Wiltshire, who can re-create cities from memory with his pen:

> The crowd in the museum
>   has come to gawk
> at the effete spectacle:
>   a working-class black man
> turned robotic scrivener.
>   What the audience
> doesn't understand is that Stephen
>   has already swum away;
> in his place a more substantial
>   cloud of blackened mucus,
> a spectral Houdini.[1]

Both Lonnie and DJ's Stephen are forced to disappear from systemically distorted and distorting eyes, utilizing the obscurity blackness affords—*a blackish purple*—to escape. There is dignity in camouflage, in the strategic disappearance and re-appearance ink provides. When the ink of others, especially in representing who you are, seems always to smear and run errant, it becomes necessary to take the pen and write your own story.

And that's what happened, in a radical manner, midway through the year. Lonnie and I had gathered with Erin, his insightful and supportive teacher, in a conference room where we could minimize the impact of others. Lonnie sat down and declared, unequivocally, that there would be no writing today. I closed my laptop and asked Lonnie if there was anything troubling him. He crossed his arms, "People are stupid." I nodded. "I just wish they would ask the right questions," he continued. I knew the feeling. "Yeah," I replied, "sometimes people think they understand me when I know they don't." But I could see my sympathy wasn't making things better. "I bet you know the right questions," I hazarded. Lonnie looked at me intensely. "I often interview people," I continued. "Perhaps I could help you interview yourself?" He smiled slightly and said, "I could do that."

The only question I asked was, "What's the first question you wish someone would ask?" After that, Lonnie dove in, asking and answering the questions himself, while I dictated, struggling to keep up:

How did you get taken away?

When I was young and I was seven years old, my mom did bad stuff. She needed help. She needed treatment. The last time I visited her I was seven and I don't even remember the building.

Were you poor?

I did have a house. We didn't have a lot of food. My mom didn't have a lot of money, so she stole stuff from stores. We used to eat food at home sometimes. We had a bed, but then we moved to a new house and we didn't have a bed anymore, so we slept on clothes. We didn't have heat, but we had a heater. We had cable TV. I had some toys. It was just me and my mom. She tickled me and kissed me. She told me, "I love you." She would hold me like a baby and sing a song to me, but I don't remember the words.

Where did you go to?

I went to a shelter. I was in respite. My mom was still my guardian, but she needed help. I didn't like it because I cried a lot and missed my mom. I was hyper. I saw her picture and I cried. I liked Pam and Bob and Greg and Ben and Tito. They had fun and took me out. There were other kids too, but they weren't the same age as me. Then I went back to my mom over and over. But the court said no. Then I met my guardian, Karen Pretty.

Did you ever think you'd be back with your mom?

Yeah, I was thinking about how much I missed her and asked my guardian if I could go back with my mom. They said no. I called my mom a lot. It went for a long time. She called me, too.

How did your mom die?

I was ten years old and in foster care. I was in school. My guardian told me my mom died. I didn't believe it at first. She died of a drug overdose. My mom was depressed. She was sad because she was missing me. Then my cousin broke open the glass on her door and found her dead. They called the ambulance, but she was already dead. They wouldn't let me go to the funeral. They wouldn't let me say goodbye. It made me sad. It made me upset. I have her ashes. They are in a metal square on my dresser. I look at it and think about her a lot. She's in heaven now and she watches over me. It makes her happy.

What does your mom think about you now?

She is happy. She's proud of me. She tells me she loves me. She tells me she misses me and hugs me and kisses me on the cheek. Even though she's a spirit I can feel it. And she's in my dreams.

How did you stay strong?

I don't think about the bad things. Sometimes I do, but I know my mom needed help. I think about my life and how I wouldn't see her no more. I pray about it sometimes. I hope I get adopted by new parents. I hope they are nice and caring and help me work out my anger issues. I hope they tell me they love me and they miss me.

What do you want to do with your life?

I want to work at a group home. I want to help kids with disabilities. I'll help them clean their rooms and not think about the bad things in their lives and help them do good in their lives.

After that day, Lonnie's demeanor with me changed. Many days he was ready to write the moment I stepped in the room, even chastising me if I was a minute late. Having told his story in the way he wanted it told, Lonnie was able to assume some authority in our sessions that went beyond refusal. Having somewhat unburdened his heart, Lonnie made space for his wild imagination, which was clamoring with ideas.

This was the state of mind he inhabited one gray winter day when I walked into his classroom bemoaning the colorless drear. Lonnie took that as a challenge. I opened up my laptop and he reeled off the first stanza:

> Lonnie is blue and green and yellow
> and red and black and white

I asked him if he could make a simile, comparing each of his colors to a grounding object. No problem:

> like the sky and the earth and the grass
> and telephones and firefighters
> and a werewolf and ice cream

I asked him what he would do if there were a way to give today's sky his colors:

> Today is gray, but if Lonnie could fly
> she would fly a rainbow into the sky
> and become Rainbow Man

Our time was almost up, so I read the poem aloud for Lonnie and asked whether he'd like to make any changes. After he confirmed everything was to his liking, I asked Lonnie if we could continue exploring this character next week. "I really want to know more about Rainbow Man," I said, raising my eyebrows. Lonnie's aide, Farrah, who'd become a crucial supporter, nodded and said, "Me too."

When I stepped back into Lonnie's classroom a week later, it was clear that he'd been thinking about Rainbow Man all week. The moment I sat down he surprised me with an unexpected revelation: "Rainbow Man is a wrestler." I'd been expecting a superhero but was immediately ready to follow Lonnie into the ring. Looking back on it now, the figure of the professional wrestler seems like a strategic choice, as he can present a more complex take on gender. While superheroes often counterpoise their strength with ambivalence, or even reluctance, wrestlers shamelessly foreground their masculinity, even while primping and posing in formfitting singlets, their muscled frames often topped by a cascade of flaxen locks à la Hulk Hogan. They partake in a flamboyant form of gender fluidity while somehow reinforcing the masculine. Now I don't mean to suggest that Lonnie was or is even remotely similar to a wrestler in these respects—in fact, he is habitually neutral when it comes to the visual performance of gender—but the wrestler's unflagging devotion to masculinity might have been a beacon of sorts for Lonnie at that moment, an aspirational talisman that helped him envision *him*.

As if to bolster this gender paradigm, Lonnie immediately introduced the contrasting character of Wonder Woman Rainbow, based loosely on Farrah. Let's examine Lonnie's poem two stanzas at a time:

Rainbow Man Enters the Ring

In jean shorts and a gold chain
with a rainbow colored headband
and rainbow Jordans with rainbow socks
and a rainbow t-shirt with a big R
over his six-pack and big muscles

Then his sidekick, Wonder Woman Rainbow,
enters the ring wearing a short rainbow cape
and a rainbow mask and matching rainbow Jordans
with rainbow shorts and rainbow gloves
and a rainbow belt with a big R on the buckle

Though you can't see it here, Lonnie insisted that the title of his poem be laid out in Rainbow Man's vibrant array of colors. Lonnie picked out these colors specifically and suggested we return to the original Rainbow Man poem to retrofit that title with colors as well. As this matching tag team enters the ring, Lonnie presents the reader with a detailed description, every aspect of their twinned ensembles working to emphasize a vivid swagger. But every main event needs its villain, so along comes Black Scarecrow:

When his opponent, Black Scarecrow,
charged at him, Rainbow Man shot red
fire from his hands and Black Scarecrow's
face turned red with anger

Black Scarecrow charged again
and Rainbow Man dodged,
but Black Scarecrow grabbed
Wonder Woman Rainbow

There is no escaping the parallel between Lonnie's octopus, which turns red to scare other animals, and Black Scarecrow, whose "face turns red with anger" in this third stanza. Given

the parallel, I'd argue there's a strong chance that Black
Scarecrow isn't a villain at all but has merely inherited that
role, or had it thrust upon him, as the story lines of pro-
fessional wrestling often leverage and hyperbolize society's
latent nationalism and racism, turning it blatant and theatri-
cal. Luckily, Rainbow Man knows how to harness more than
anger:

Rainbow Man shot Black Scarecrow
full of dark pink and he was
filled with love

Wonder Woman Rainbow
kissed him so hard he flew down
to the mat and when he asked her
to marry him she said Yes!

What a twist! Rainbow Man's superpower seems to entail
some melding of the octopus and the amygdala, as if a ceph-
alopod's lightning quick chromatophores were enhanced with
emotional charge and given projectile force. I love how Lon-
nie, who is often said to struggle with emotional intelligence,
has chosen emotion as a cornerstone for Rainbow Man's core
ability. And I also love how the thinly veiled theater of profes-
sional wrestling here devolves or transforms into pure theater,
like an avant-garde restaging of *The Taming of the Shrew*. Can
you imagine the ratings if WWE were to use this story line at
WrestleMania? The wedding, however, is the real prime-time
event:

> Rainbow Man was the priest
> and performed the marriage
> and Black Scarecrow also wanted
> Rainbow Man to be his best man

> Rainbow Man invited all his wrestler friends
> like Lightning the Cheetah and Sharkboy
> and Darkness and Blue Octopus

Lonnie conjures a menagerie of wrestling comrades. Lightning the Cheetah and Sharkboy are sleek and predatory, while Blue Octopus hearkens back to Lonnie's first poem. Darkness exceeds the animal frame, a character seemingly constructed of nothing but the specter of all that is dark. But clearly "all that is dark," in the world of this poem, is not unwelcome. Darkness is literally *invited* to the wedding, offered the hospitality of friends who gather to celebrate love. But like a garish reality show, drama unfolds quickly:

> They partied so hard that Black Scarecrow
> said Rainbow Man ruined the wedding
> but Rainbow Man said it was the best party ever
> And Wonder Woman Rainbow agreed

> Rainbow Man started rapping
> I'm cooler than everybody and full of color
> I'm awesome and got more muscles than any other

So perhaps Rainbow Man isn't as deft with emotions as we had hoped, sloughing his duties as officiant and best man in order to better embrace his inner libertine. With characteristic Lonnie flare, Rainbow Man has the last word. How's this for a devastating mic drop:

> Scarecrow said it's not always about you!
> It's about me and Wonder Woman right now

> But Rainbow Man didn't care
> He was having too much fun and said
> I only came for the food

Despite the truth in Scarecrow's exasperated claim, sometimes it *is* all about you. Lonnie needed a figure that could demonstrate self-realization with glorious abandon, no matter what other people thought. Lonnie forged Rainbow Man into an unlikely role model, giving broad permission for the legitimacy of Lonnie's inner world and his desired transformation. After that day, Lonnie asked that everyone refer to him as a boy or a man. Three years later he would publish a chapbook of poems titled *Ode to Every Black Boy*, a celebration of the resilience and artistry of Black boys everywhere and in every form. For a while he even became Dwight, a name he felt better embodied his newly revealed self. But then he returned to Lonnie. In all other ways he remained the person I met at the beginning of the school year, except now he seemed more bold, more confident, more *him*.

No matter what the future holds, Lonnie now has a way to articulate who he is, where he's been, and what he's becoming. When people stare at him, as they will inevitably continue to do, I hope Lonnie's poems fill him with protective resilience, a bright energy fueled by his inner Rainbow Man. For Lonnie, truth is synonymous with expression, and every week that we meet to write poems is an opportunity for him to reconnect with his truth and share it with others:

My Life

At 10 I knew I had special feelings for girls
but I didn't know what that meant

At 13 I decided I wanted to be a guy
and so I started wearing boy clothes
but no one in my group home supported me
They said I should wear girl clothes
so I shaved all my hair off

At 16 my friends and family weren't accepting who I was
They said I should wear girl clothes and my hair long
but I was not going to listen
I just tell the truth about who I am
It's my life

Now I'm 17 and I hate wearing girl pants
I've been researching gender
and I've learned that there are other people who feel like me
Some people even change their bodies
and take hormones
and I think that's cool
but I hate shots!

I changed my name from Lonnae
to Dwight to Jackson to Lonnie
Inside I feel like a guy
even though I look like a girl
and my voice sounds like a girl
so I thought I should change my name

I might go back to Dwight
because it sounds cooler
and it feels more me

Living in a State of Hell

Not Even Good Morning—They Break You Down—A
Promise We Can Keep—Complex Solidarities—A Kissing
Volcano—Reinventing Every Period—The Most Pleasing
Network—Ground Down to Grow Up—Give the Police
Departments to the Grandmothers

Although Lonnie gradually let me get to know the real him, it took time, and even after three years of working with him, I find that Lonnie is quick to let me know I have only scratched the surface. Here is one of my favorite poems from Lonnie's second chapbook, *Trayvon Martin*:

All the Things Chris Doesn't Know

He doesn't know my favorite color

He doesn't know the history
of the painting of the woman
who told someone to kill a guy
instead of getting married to him

He doesn't know how to live
in a group home his whole life

He doesn't know you'll be better off
if you just stay in your room
and don't say nothing
not even good morning

He doesn't know that to survive
in a group home you just eat dinner
and listen to your staff

He doesn't know my favorite basketball team
and that Steph Curry is more handsome than him
and can shoot three-pointers better than him

He doesn't know I love to play laser tag

He doesn't know I'm going to open
a new kind of YMCA for Black people
and Brown people and teenagers
and it's going to be a community center
I name after Trayvon Martin

My first week at the South Education Center, in the same residency through which I first met Mark, I also encountered a student named Soren. I had been given a heads-up by administrators that Soren, a young teenager at the time, had experienced some things (the nature of which they could only be vague about) that caused him to distrust anyone new. They hoped I might be able to engage him with poetry but also felt like it might not be a realistic expectation. The plan was for me to join Soren on one of his many daily walks around the school property, always accompanied by his educational assistant, a talented graphic artist with an impressive poker face.

Our first forty-five minutes together set the pattern: Soren spent the time testing me with provocative questions, most of which involved some variety of arson, while the EA and I attempted to draw him into other topics or model a more open exchange. Each of the next two walks played out the same way: Soren would ply me with nightmarish scenarios, and I would cling to some striking detail—a word, an image, an idea—fruitlessly attempting to turn its imaginative power toward an exit door we could walk through together. A difficult rhythm resulted—pull/push or push/pull—leaving us just where we started out and exhausting me in the process. Even so, I had come to feel more comfortable around Soren, whose attempts to keep us from having an open conversation or writing a poem were consistent in their way, and understandable, since those weren't his goals. Along the way this rhythm grew less overwhelming and slowly revealed a bright and sensitive young man working with plenty of imaginative resources.

Our fourth and final walk began the same way as the other three. I had hoped that our time together might have created the opportunity for writing, but my expectations for what form our work together could take still seemed far from Soren's concerns. Like so many students before, Soren was allowing me to learn how (and how *not*) to begin a genuine dialogue. Unfortunately, it was not a lesson I had the resources for in that moment. Frustrated that we would miss our opportunity to write, and perhaps frustrated that I had endured so much difficulty without reward, frustrated (and here is the real core of it) that I was not a good enough teacher or human being to draw Soren out—I finally gave in and let the pot (or should I say poet?) boil over: "Soren, the way you talk about the world, it's like the whole thing is on fire." I paused for a moment. "It's like we're living in hell."

Soren stopped walking. His eyes turned to mine for the first time and his face softened, the tension of his customary swagger falling away. Before he spoke I could sense that he was present—that a truly unprotected layer of Soren had revealed itself for the first time in our month of walks. His eyes widened and he asked, with absolute earnestness, "How do we know we're not?"

Though I could sense something like this was coming, I was nonetheless agape at his breathtaking question. I turned my hands palms up and answered honestly, "We don't." Soren had been describing some half-baked hell to me for an entire month, inviting me to set the world aflame, but the moment he asked his question we both knew that the inferno was redundant. No matter what anyone said, we were indeed living in hell. It was the only possible answer. Why else would a child see the things that Soren had seen? Why else would the random circumstances of one's birth determine so much of one's pain and one's possibilities? The two of us spent the next half hour talking like giddy teenagers, laughing unself-consciously about all the stupid shit people were doing—that *we* were doing—while living in hell. We started to make a list: trying new flavors of yogurt, arguing about barely discernable musical genres, recommitting to better habits that would surely allow us to reap earthly success. It was one of the most raucously cathartic conversations I've ever had.

By the time we returned to the classroom, I suggested he could turn this burgeoning list of absurdities into a poem. To my surprise, Soren was immediately on board. I quickly detailed a poem by Ted Berrigan called "Things to Do in Providence" and read him a section. I suggested he could write "Things to Do in Hell." At this point, our time together was almost gone, but Soren didn't seem too worried about getting the poem finished. He was enjoying himself, and I wasn't going to imperil that by rushing him through the composition, no matter how much I loved where he seemed to be headed. When the bell rang, his EA suggested that he and Soren could work on the poem that afternoon and promised to send it to me when it was complete. I gave Soren an awkward but joyous high five and left the room feeling hopeful.

The finished poem never materialized, and when I returned in the fall to teach another residency at SEC, I noticed that Soren wasn't on the roster of students. I ran into his EA in the hall and asked him what had happened. He didn't know any details but heard that Soren had been placed in a juvenile detention center. I was heartbroken, worried about what had become of him, what new kinds of carceral hells he might be facing. His revelation had been on my mind all summer, as wildfires swept the nation and the president of the United States relentlessly fomented racial tensions. I was so grateful to Soren: for pushing me toward hard questions, for opening up to me in return, for gifting me a framework through which I could reflect on the seemingly endless parade of pain and tragedy making its way through all of our lives. Of course, Soren's experience of all this was something I could only guess at now, but I prayed, in my secular way, that he was safe, or safe enough, and that his voice was finding other avenues to reveal all he had to offer.

I resolved to write a poem for him, a companion version of the poem he never finished, a poem (featuring a Kierkegaard reference in homage to Soren) that would eventually be the heart of my next full-length collection. I called the book *Things to Do in Hell* and thanked Soren in the acknowledgments for planting the first infernal seed. This is only one example of a student influencing my own work as a poet. And the influence that conversation has had on me as a person is far greater.

Things to Do in Hell

Grab lunch
Polish your silver
Try a new flavor of yogurt
Burn in a lake of fire
Smoke some weed
Overeat

Finally understand some things
Talk to Steve
Cry out breathlessly
Pay the electric bill
Go to the aquarium in the mall
Worry over the shape and color of your moles

Sell out the people you used to call friends
Learn how to bake bread
Feed the ducks at the lake by the highway
Exaggerate your assets
Get elected
Mull things over

Attend a livestock auction
Pull down the statues of people who tortured your ancestors
Seek employment
Knit
Regret mostly everything
Paint the windows shut

Pull down the statues of your ancestors
Get down on your knees
Read Kierkegaard
Pick the kids up from Montessori
Lose your appetite
Linger

DVR *Homeland*
Imagine that hell is only an abstraction
Take another free breath mint
Cry out endlessly
Blame those closest to you
Love even the barest light pissing through the trees

Several years later, I was walking through the halls of SEC and heard someone say the name Soren. I tracked them down: "Did you just say 'Soren'?" The look in my eye must have been pretty intense, because they flinched a little before replying that, yes, they had just seen Soren walking around the building. I ran down the stairs and outside. I kept running around the building until I saw a tall, lanky, bearded young man who looked like he could be Soren walking and talking with the same EA from long ago. It's like they'd never stopped, and yet Soren had aged immensely.

As we began catching up, I realized he'd matured in other ways as well. He was thrilled to hear about my poem and the forthcoming book he had inspired. We talked about Nietzsche and depression and his newfound love of rap. He had no idea I was also a rapper and so we spit bars back and forth for a while.

The last I heard Soren was back in juvie. I have written at length here of the way poetry offers the possibilities of structure and pattern to help facilitate neurodivergent poets. But we cannot forget how the entwined structures of ableism and white supremacy lead to other unmistakable patterns, especially the patterns of violence toward and institutionalization of Black and disabled and neurodivergent individuals. Lonnie and Soren surely don't forget it. The city of Minneapolis will not, I hope, forget it any time soon. Nor Denver, nor Milwaukee, nor Chicago, nor America, nor the world. And while I'm not sure where Soren is right now or why, I can say with confidence that we're all still in hell, trying new flavors of yogurt and fighting as hard as we can to write and learn and love our way out. At least we get to be here together.

. . .

In the midst of writing this book, my neighborhood of South Minneapolis became the epicenter of a racial justice uprising that inspired action and change throughout the world. It took just under nine minutes for white Minneapolis police officer Derek Chauvin to brutally and impassively murder George Floyd (while three of Chauvin's peers actively chose not to intervene), and then it took just over a week for the Minneapolis City Council (including Black trans councilwoman and poet Andrea Jenkins) to announce its plans to defund the Minneapolis

Police Department. In that officer's face I instantly recognized a blank, disassociated veneer of dominion that makes this kind of unthinkable violence commonplace in America. It's a look I've witnessed countless times, on the faces of boys and men who look like me, since I was a child. It is a sickness sunk down deep in the body.[1] It is a sickness predicated on the idea that one body (white, male, cis, straight, rich, able) is "normal" and every other body will be measured against it, diminishing in value as it strays from that false norm.

And too often it is someone who looks like me who will explain or narrate disabled and racialized lives. As Lonnie demonstrated in his self-interview, there is immense power in reclaiming the narrative of one's own life. I wrote the essay that makes up the bulk of the previous chapter nearly two years before George Floyd's murder. Since then, Lonnie has deepened into his identity as a Black trans activist and produced dozens of poems that voice the complexity of living a variously inter-sected life. As the Uprising for racial justice spiraled around my neighborhood, as I made my nightly pre-curfew reconnais-sance for unmarked cars used by white supremacists to ferry accelerants, as I held midnight vigils against those same white supremacist agitators, a question from Lonnie's poem "They Break You Down" spiraled around my mind: "And what if you're Black / *and* have a disability?" I felt so grateful to have Lonnie's poem and the permission to share it during those weeks. I sent it out to hundreds of people through my newsletter on the morning of Friday, May 29, 2020, and it was shared with thousands more.

They Break You Down

When you lose your parent
and the state "takes care" of you
they break you down

They hire someone to control you
because of the color of your skin
and they break you down

You lose your rights and your voice
when they break you down

You try to prove them wrong
but they only look at your past

You're weak, you're depressed
you're tired, you're stressed

Living in the hands of the state
is living in a state of hell

What does your guardian
guard you from?
The truth

What does the state state?
Nothing

They dodge everything:
the truth, the question, my history
all the ways I've changed

And what if you're Black
and have a disability?
They break you down

I know so many people with disabilities
that are smart and have something inside them
but they don't have a voice

But they *do* have a voice
Don't let them break you down

For many young people like Lonnie there are hells within hells. Living Black in America is a kind of hell.[2] But what if you are Black *and* a ward of the state? What if you are Black *and* a ward of the state *and* trans *and* neurodivergent? In a poem from *Trayvon Martin*, Lonnie actually writes "I *am* Hell. I own the place." The inherently violent framework of systemic racism that pervades policing also pervades foster care and group homes and health care and our public school system. It takes tremendous resilience to survive in the folds of these overlapping hells, where someone always seems poised to break you down.

Lonnie's voice is the key to his resilience, and his poems have become a beacon for others, both those who share his experiences and those who don't. When it comes to the latter group, Lonnie is an educator. His intersectional identity is at the core of his ability to teach. Because Lonnie has faced prejudice on multiple fronts, he has been forced to develop resources for confronting the inner workings of society with a directness and clarity that few can rival. This is a central tenet of standpoint theory, coined by feminist and philosopher Sandra Harding to describe how those who claim the least inherited power are able to perceive the dynamics of power most clearly.[3] As a person who has been positioned by history to inherit the *most* power, I've spent most of my life misapprehending the truth about patriarchy and systemic racism, navigating my way through a dense hegemonic fog that desires always to keep the dynamics of power invisible. Though I can't strip privilege from my body, I have labored to slough endless layers of it from my thinking, to see things as they actually are.

Lonnie, on the other hand, sees and speaks truth with tremendous clarity. To survive, he has had to be an autodidact, a self-educating scholar of power and its effects. And that's why, nearly a month after the murder of George Floyd, Lonnie, one of the most vulnerable students at the South Education Center, a school for some of the most vulnerable students in the Twin Cities, was asked to read his poems at a public meeting of the School Board. Dozens and dozens of lifelong educators, tireless administrators, and lifesaving social workers gathered in their Zoom boxes to learn from Lonnie. Here is the first poem he read:

Ode

Ode to the fact
that I am a Black boy

Ode to every Black boy
to the living and dead
but especially the living

Ode to the ones going to college
and playing football
and being who they are
and not letting people get to them
even the racists

Ode to the Black boys
who don't stop
and who stay proud

Ode to the Black boys
who see other Black boys
getting shot
and getting abandoned

Ode to the Black boys
in foster care
who survive everything

Ode to the Black boys
who get really angry
and think no one cares
and find someone to support them

Ode to the Black boys
who tell their own stories

Ode to the Black boys
who can still do it
who are smart
and artistic

Ode to the Black boys
who are artists

I see them
I am proud of us
and we're all
gonna find somebody
to love us

In the wake of an unparalleled global uprising demanding justice and an end to racialized violence, Lonnie wasn't out for retribution or revenge. Lonnie wanted the boys like him to be seen. Lonnie wanted the boys like him to be loved. And despite everything he's been through, Lonnie remains certain that love is a promise we make to each other. A promise we can keep. Even in hell.

. . .

Hannah Emerson, denizen of the listening world, has a different standpoint from Lonnie. She is white and she is nonspeaking. But like Lonnie, Hannah has had to reckon with a system that set out to change who she was or deny it altogether. Despite early experiences within the punitive and demeaning structures of behavior modification that so many nonspeaking autists endure, Hannah has interdependently forged a life that can encompass a more abundant range of who she is and wants to be. I believe that's why her poems, written before and after the Uprising, speak so powerfully alongside Lonnie's, creating complementary and complex solidarities.

I was prepared for the ways in which Lonnie and Hannah might harmonize, because hell shows up with some regularity in Hannah's writing. I'm thinking especially of her definition of autism: "Please get this hell is mine. It is great life of trying to be here, because I help the world get that they need to become me to help themselves." Hannah has found a way to revel in the staring that can, as Lonnie confirmed in his first poem, really sting. Having been branded an outsider, she has claimed that mantle with purpose, recognizing within the struggle of "trying to be here" the power to show "helpful people" another way. Hannah is nothing if not generous, but that doesn't mean she will protect us from the reckoning we need to face, nor from the fact that we will need to face it together.

The Monday after the Uprising began, having read Lonnie's poems in my latest newsletter, Hannah was moved to write not one but two poems, one laborious letter at a time, in our one-hour session. Here is the first, which furthermore resonates with the volcanic forgings of Sid, Mark, and Max:

How the World Began

Please try to cut
yourself open
to find the blood
that is the color
of the molten rock

that is in all of us
yes—please try
to help the world
by heaving your
hatred on the flames
that burn in your town
yes yes—please try
to melt yes yes—please
try to grow into the stream
of molten life yes yes—please
try to help us make kissing
kissing volcano that loves
with way of floating hell
that we are now now
now yes yes yes—
please get that this
is how the world
began began
began yes yes

Far from being a "melting pot" of post-racial delusion, the molten core of this poem portrays the current moment as a rupture with all that came before. Hell is not a prison to Hannah but a place where new possibilities are forged. This transformation is echoed in her strategic use of "yes yes," which falls where a period otherwise might. She writes:

My yes gives me my signature yes. My yes gives me grownding yes yes. My yes gives me the energy to be me yes yes. Please get that the yes yes is me going for it.

Please get that I have been waiting my whole life for this life to become freedom through my words nothing helping me become them keeping them inside me hurt my soul yes yes. Keeping just hurt my great great great soul yes yes. Please get that I love my life now yes yes. Please get that I help everyone by being me yes yes. Please get that this is being great brave to go to nothing yes yes.

Hannah's "yes yes" allows her to find flow with the desires of her bodymind, her own volcanic alapa body. Imagine reinventing every period as the words "yes yes." Imagine taking every period-shaped bullet hole that stops a life and doubling that life's affirmation. Imagine saying "no" so loud that it becomes the double yes of a new world sprouting in every direction.

This is the bravery that Hannah brings to her poems, an unflinching commitment to face the nothing, the hell, whatever container we can construct for the negative imaginary. And then to find there the seeds that we need to begin again. To quote a poem, "Revolutionary Letter #10," by Diane di Prima, which Hannah is familiar with:

These are transitional years and the dues
will be heavy.
Change is quick but revolution
will take a while.
America has not even begun as yet.
This continent is seed.[4]

Hannah is a revolutionary writer, unafraid to hold the space where kissing meets the volcano.

The second poem Hannah wrote that day follows from the
first:

The Underworld

Let's try to go
to the underworld
that melts us
into one yes
yes—love the mystery
that is there yes
yes—love the network
that is trying to connect
us yes yes—love
the most pleasing
network that grows
there yes yes—please
try to become the lovely
thoughts that are born
there yes yes—please
try to become the great
great great life that grows
from there yes yes—please
try to kiss the smelly
sweetness that is
there yes yes—please
please please grow
into the sweetness
that the universe wants
you to be be be be be

yes yes yes—please
try to understand that
you must grow down
to grow up yes yes

Just as Hannah subverts our notions of hell, she here re-
frames the underworld as a network of harmonic connection.
In other words, she reminds us of what the underworld really is,
a mycelium-based wonder of unfathomable complexity and rhi-
zomatic growth. We must, as Rimbaud once wrote, "return to
the soil seeking obligation." If we are to belong to each other, we
must belong to the land first. A property mindset, rather than
tying us to the land, is actually the first thing that separates us
from it. This is a basic tenet of the Dakota people, whose stolen
land I myself live on. The land doesn't belong to us; we belong
to the land.

When Hannah merges "grow" and "ground" into her hy-
brid signifier *grownd*, she reminds us how movement is never
only in one direction. Grownd is a verb and a noun simultane-
ously, an action and a state, meaning growth that is insepara-
ble from the land, from history (which lives in the land), and
from our obligation to live in relation to the land, one being
among many. As Resmaa Menakem and other facilitators of
healing have shown, grounding is an irreplaceable part of one's
liberation. White bodies and Black bodies both need to heal
from racial and historical trauma, and these bodies, *our* bodies,
require grounding to help us metabolize and unlearn what has
been passed down to us. My autistic students understand this.
Grownding is an essential part of their ability to participate in
the social world every single day. From a corporeal perspective,

their experiences have made them standpoint experts on how the body can grow down to grow up.

And let us not forget pleasure! As Hannah's anaphoric *please* repeatedly emphasizes, we must find pleasure in the process. When you have done the grownding work of racial justice, you discover a "most pleasing network." Liberation can seem almost impossibly difficult, but its rewards are real. They are authentic. And I love how my autistic students demand authenticity. Once you can acknowledge that we are all living in hell, that we have been burning down our own house for as long as America has existed, that we have inherited an unspeakable trauma that society conditions us to ignore and bury, that we must not only think *but act* out of this knowledge, that we must return to our bodies and having returned there we must return to the soil, then you can finally "kiss the smelly sweetness" of liberation, which is not separate from obligation yes yes / we are an interdependent network of bodies, human and more-than-human yes yes / we are the pliant web of love that the universe desires into being yes yes.

. . .

One of my favorite local poets and pleasure activists is Junauda Petrus-Nasah. When Minneapolis City Council members took that first step toward an anti-racist and police-free future, they asked Junauda to close the ceremony. She wrote her poem "Could We Please Give the Police Stations to the Grandmothers" in 2015 after the murderer of Michael Brown was not indicted, and police abolitionists have acknowledged it as a key factor in allowing them to imagine a way forward. As the City Council ceded the stage to Junauda and she began to read, I thought of Lonnie and I thought of Hannah and I thought of all of us entangled in the smelly sweetness of transforming our world. I encourage you to go to a computer right now and find a video of Junauda reading this poem, but here's an excerpt just in case:

Grandma is a sacred child herself, who just circled the sun
  enough times into the ripeness of her cronehood.
She wants your life to be sweeter.

When you wildin' out because your heart is broke or you
  don't have what you need, the grandmas take your hand
  and lead you to their gardens. You can lay down amongst
  the flowers. Her grasses, roses, dahlias, irises, lilies, collards,
  kale, eggplants, blackberries. She wants you to know that
  you are safe and protected, universal, limitless, sacred,
  sensual, divine and free.

Grandma is the original warrior, wild since birth, comfortable
  in loving fiercely. She has fought so that you don't have to,
  not in the same ways at least.

So give the police departments to the grandmas, they are fear-
  less, classy and actualized. Blossomed from love.[5]

Calm-Arriving to a Wanting Safe World

My Mind Is Prodigious—My Love Is Extravagant—
Billowing—From Patter to Pattern—Hard Landings and
Good Days—Held in Nature—Disability Is an Art—
Simmering in Our Homes—We Are Better as a Community

I hear the familiar Skype jingle and run a hand through my hair. When I accept the call, Zach's pixilated face coheres on-screen, accompanied by Larysa, his adept communication partner. His hands are busy with colorful beads, like the kind worn at Mardi Gras, and he diligently wraps them in elaborate convolutions around his left hand. Zach, nonspeaking and expressive, intermittently permits sly smiles to emerge from his customary half-scowl of concentration. In Chapter 3 we discovered how much Zach perceived of his housemate and friend Bill. We know now that autists like Zach, given the right supports, are richly communicative and live lives of deep sociality, often surrounded by incredible collaborators who help them encounter the demands of a complex world built without them in mind. While many autists struggle with (or against) normative social expectations, they often find themselves enmeshed in mutual relationships that challenge hollow notions of independence, actively embracing a lively interdependence instead.

Today Zach is writing a poem about the word "great," but the necessity to write this poem is anything but. His parents asked whether he would write an elegy for his brother, who tragically passed away the week before. At the time of this tragedy, Zach and I had been working together for only a few weeks, but already poetry had established itself as a unique vehicle for Zach's most complex feelings. Many called Zach's brother's death a "great" loss and this confused Zach, who perceived a word like "great" as hurtfully misplaced in this particular context. In processing disconnects like these, he's found writing to be helpful, so we begin by looking up the word "great" in a thesaurus. We set aside a pool of synonyms as reference material for his poem. When Zach indicates his desire for a helping prompt, I suggest a possibility for how the line might begin. Then Zach, with Larysa's help, writes whatever feels most vital to him, typing one assisted letter at a time. She supports his elbow and forearm with her hands, resetting his posture between letters, giving him a calm launching pad to engage his linguistic focus. He chooses the phrase "I think" to anchor the beginning of the first three lines:

I think my Daddy is great
I think my brother is awesome
I think my mind is prodigious

Like other autistic writers, Zach uses this anaphoric anchor to propel and structure his thoughts. He begins the poem with a characteristic trope in his work: his love for his father. The second line seems to continue in the same vein, but given Zach's recent loss, I feel the awful side of awe nesting inside awesome. When Zach chooses "prodigious" as the descriptor for his mind in the third line, I am quietly delighted. The word choice itself, among all the other possible synonyms for "great" he might have chosen, demonstrates its truth. Zach's mind *is* prodigious, especially when you realize that in another era (or even in this one, if he weren't blessed with dedicated parents and access to critical resources) he might have been thought incapable of communication and relegated to a life of isolation. This is where terms like "low-functioning" lose their meaning. A prodigious mind is definitively not a low-functioning one. A prodigious mind has sensitive resources galore.

For the next lines Zach chooses to shift our anaphoric phrase to "I know" and continues typing with an expression of deep and hardwon concentration:

I know my love is extravagant
I know my brother passing is terrible
I know that winter is crazy
I know you are happy

Zach's love *is* extravagant. He writes about his love often, and its frequency never diminishes the effect it has on his loved ones, who are bathed anew each time with its glow. He knows that his love makes a difference. In the history of autism, this certitude has been at stake in the very definition of whether an autistic person is worthy of care, of services, and, most crucially, of reciprocal love. What would happen if our contemporary society could agree, at minimum, that love is both a practice and feeling intrinsic to autistic experience, regardless of how it is or is not made perceptible? When we doubt that others can love, we doubt that they are fundamentally human. And we begin to cast doubt on our own ability to love.

The fifth line speaks for itself. It is the place where some terrific force grows terrible, where great love becomes great loss. It's enough to make one feel crazy, a feeling embodied in the sixth line by winter in its swirling and grave cacophony. And yet there's something inherently humorous about this sixth line. Both Larysa and I laugh, the bubble of grief popped momentarily, and Zach's smile briefly emerges. With this acknowledgment of how grief can lead to laughter, to release, the poem gains momentum. Larysa asks Zach how he knows I am happy. He writes, "Because your smile is bright." Zach, despite his supposed difficulty reading social cues and body language, has done exactly that. Over the digital divide that separates us, he's used my face to do far more than decode my emotions; he's generously allowed them to amplify the light of this already bright poem. I ask Zach if it makes sense for him to include that explanation in the poem, and he confirms that it does.

These lines, on their own, would be enough to make most of us reconsider what a young man said to have "classic autism" can understand and express, if not who he fundamentally is—but the next line is why I can't stop thinking about this particular poem and the circumstances of its composition. Without prompting, Zach signaled his desire to type and then returned to the earlier "I think" mode of the poem's beginning: "I think my Daddy is . . ." As the last word began to materialize, "b-i-l-l," Larysa's first instinct was that Zach had lost focus, because sometimes he would type Bill's name when that happened. So she asked him to start over. When he began again the same way, "b-i-l-l,"

Larysa asked him to start over once more. Writing through and with the sensorimotor challenges of autism can require extraordinary acts of concentration, so it's no wonder that communication partners are looking for the moments when a writer seems to drift, but sometimes this well-meaning vigilance can shield them from an unexpected path. So when Zach returned to the same pattern of letters a third time, I wanted to see where it was going. I asked Larysa to let him continue uninterrupted, and out came "billowing." As you might imagine, "billowing" was nowhere to be found in our lists of synonyms for "great." It's a word that rarely appears unless you're hanging laundry or standing on the deck of a sailboat.[1] I sat with it for a moment, taking in the full sensory experience of billowing in all its unexpected strangeness.

That's when it hit me. My eyes involuntarily started to well up. What I heard in that line was that Zach's dad, in the throes of an incalculable grief, was *billowing*. Stripped hollow by the tragedy of a lost child, the wind of grief was passing through him, turning his entire being into a rending tremble. I reflected my understanding of the line back to Zach, who made his particular sound of confirmation, which sounds something like the conventional *mm-hmm*. Larysa, listening, joined me in tears. The truth is, I'm not sure I have ever heard a more embodied statement of how grief feels. I may never know exactly what Zach meant by billowing, and he, like many poets before him, may not want to thoroughly explain his choice, for fear of minimizing the possibility of interpretation, but the emotional acuity of Zach's line, to my ear, continues to stagger me each time I think about it.

This is only one of the prodigious elements that characterize

Zach's mind and the minds of many of his nonspeaking peers. They feel emotions deeply, and if given the right supports to overcome the sensorimotor obstacles they have for expressing them, they can illustrate the embodied experience of emotions in a way few can match. Zach billows me with his abilities, and since he wrote this poem I have returned to it over and over when I encounter deep grief or am helping someone else work through it.

As Zach nears the end of his poem, I know he's going to want to stop at ten lines. He has a thing about the number ten. He likes to count it over and over again, feeling the wave of numbers rise in excitement to meet that double digit. When the sensorimotor complexity inside his body reaches a crescendo, he often breaks from the letters on his keyboard and types the numbers, one through ten, over and over, as a way of regaining his calm. As such, he often ends his poems at the tenth line, and this poem was no exception. He changed our focus one last time and began the line with the words "I imagine," completing it in his ever-hopeful way: "I imagine god's place is lovely." Here is the poem in its throttling entirety:

I Think, I Know, I Imagine

I think my Daddy is great
I think my brother is awesome
I think my mind is prodigious
I know my love is extravagant
I know my brother passing is terrible
I know that winter is crazy
I know you are happy

Because your smile is bright
I think my Daddy is billowing
I imagine god's place is lovely

Like Hannah writing about "things that live / in deep hurt" or Lonnie writing about "the Black boys / who tell their own stories" or Zach writing about his father's "billowing" grief, neurodivergent writers often seek out the page when they want to process a world that too closely resembles hell. They are prodigious at finding words for tragedy, even if it's a tragedy that's still unfolding, nebulous and beguiling. When the pandemic began, I knew my students would have words for the experience of it that I couldn't find. On one hand, my students, especially the ones with intense sensorimotor challenges, are more vulnerable during a pandemic, given that they sometimes have a greater need for medical intervention and rely on structured educational environments to provide much of their intellectual and social enrichment. They often feel isolated and anxious during the most "normal" of times. On the other hand, this is exactly what has prepared them to lead during a destabilizing moment like this. They have, essentially, been studying and developing and practicing ways to cope with anxiety and isolation their whole lives. They have been learning how to ground themselves, calm themselves, move toward hope, and focus on love.

In my first session with Adam Wolfond after the pandemic began, he typed: "How I mostly think about this time is always fearful. I am always wondering when I am calm-arriving to a wanting safe world." I replied that many people I know have found themselves stuck in a fear-loop, wondering what's happening and what's to come. But I also noted how Adam, in my experience, has been practicing this "calm-arriving" for a very long time and diligently articulating the "wanting safe world" in his poems. He agreed that he was poised at this moment to help others, having worked so hard to help himself. With this exchange, he began typing:

Isolation Song of Love

Isolation is the way I am
thinking about how people
are with each other and I am
thinking about how always
the people want me to stay

away. I am good at really

staying away from people
wanting laurels of sowed
speed of speech about too
willful bodies together
assembling meaning.

The willful people are those
who fiat the way of pleasing
freedom. Very leading
leaders want to wash
the waters of freedom

away and want us to

language everything in
the words of politics. I am
languaging my way the long
poetic feelings packing
together the pace of the world.

Adam included a space in his writing of the word "to /
gether," and when he'd placed the period after "world" I asked
him whether he wanted to emphasize that pause by splitting
the word over a line break, which he did. This question gave
us the occasion to work our way back to the beginning of the
poem, looking at formal possibilities and seizing opportuni-
ties that emerged. The first line break emphasizes the irony
in Adam's relation to isolation. He, as autistic, has had to face
misguided notions of isolation ("the way I am") baked into
the label hanging over his head. But isolation is also the way
Adam is thinking about others and the way they are constantly
agitating for space from othered bodies. As we saw in Chap-
ter 1, Adam has faced vehement discrimination from people
who didn't want someone like him in their space. This idea is
further emphasized by another ironic break, the stanza break,
opening up the chasm between "stay" and "away," words that
rhyme even as they repel.

Adam often writes about "patter" and "pattern," the latter
allowing the writer to transcend the former. We talked about
how the emerging pattern of this poem might emphasize the
sophistication of Adam's ever-moving cognition. The four five-
line stanzas of approximately equal line length separated by
the two isolated "away" stanzas create a pattern that pleases the
eye and welcomes readers in, ensuring that they know someone

has cared for the language. In this hospitable house of languaging, readers are given a loving space where they can assemble meaning alongside Adam, but only if they can slough off the fast-paced political jargon of the day and open themselves up to that more poetically paced possibility. Although in some ways Adam is more vulnerable to the restrictions of the pandemic, he is also more prepared to slow down and weather the uncertainty.

As he entered the second half of the poem, Adam picked up his languaging fluidity, the words intoned by his text-to-speech software coming at a steady stream:

I am thinking that laurels
of pace should be our language
to really free people like me.
I am language of thinking
and that paces other than fast

people Adams calmness to help
and pace others. My pace is
wanting to ground calmly like
a smooth landing. I am thinking
that the questions people have

are awkward and they say
they want the sickness to go
away but Jack of all virus
is not going soon so long
days of no answers will be

hard landings. Good days you
will have in isolation and you
will learn to be answering about
each other so the way about
isolation is the way of love.

Like Hannah, who wrote "I help the world get that they
need to become me to help themselves," Adam here is at-
tempting to teach us how to *Adam* our way toward equilib-
rium and balance, toward smooth landings. When he had
finished typing, tears were welling in my eyes, not just because
I was so proud of my student, but also because I was so grate-
ful for his wisdom and his compassion. As he shifts from his
lyrical "I" to the second-person "you," Adam creates a pow-
erful space of address. I'm slightly allergic to platitudes about
teachers learning from their students, but in this moment I
felt a nearly unspeakable gratitude for Adam's strength, his
ability to voice my deepest hopes for loving resilience amid
pandemic uncertainty. I instantly wanted to paste this poem
on every telephone pole in the neighborhood, providing at
least some alternative to the president's hollow, callous farce
of leadership.

Although there have been many hard landings in my family's
house during the pandemic, its attendant levels of intensity
and intimacy have allowed us to discover wider and deeper
territories for our love to grow into. Wilder territories, too.
My wife and I and our two young sons have, like Adam, been
drawn into the woods, following the pace of trees and rivers,
gathering sticks and listening closely. I think this expanded

practice of love played a crucial role in the Uprising as well. As the gears of the machine slowed just enough for us to hear one another again, we discovered a more-than-human world of mutual flourishing and regard. In that diffuse recommitment to love we also discovered we could no longer let the virus of racism spread unchecked. The pandemic has been an education, and I have never felt more grateful to have my prodigious students as my mentors.

The next week, I asked Adam if he'd like to continue thinking and writing about the pandemic and its effects. When he typed "yes," I recalled his words from our previous session and asked whether he could envision the "wanting safe world" he'd been wondering about.

Calm-Arriving to a Wanting Safe World

I want to write about questions
of sickness. I want to ask if we
will be okay. I really want answers
to things like always partly the need
for answers. Is the answer always
trying to reach us and is it easy?

I like the trees that answer lots
of wanting always the withheld
answers. I think that the answers
are held in nature and I think
that in the questions always we
feel lots of anxiety. The water

and the language are like answers
that love the way I am always
feeling easy when I bathe in rallying
array of leased language of talkers.
Yes the way I sway the awesome
rally is pandering the same language

but I dance it differently. I think that
I am answering in my movement I am
awkward but I can dance a lot
of thoughts at the same time. Really
think that I can dance better than
most in this time landing to the place

amazing that we are bodies
appreciating each other and thinking
about keeping everyone safe.

Much like in the previous poem, Adam found his optimum poetic fluidity about halfway through the poem's composition. And, in fully authentic Adam fashion, that optimum fluidity is heralded by the appearance of water: "The water // and the language are like answers / that love the way I am always / feeling easy when I bathe in rallying / array of leased language of talkers." Gah! A perfect three-wave Wolfond passage if there ever was one. In the midst of this isolating pandemic, Adam does what he always does: he looks to nature—a nature that is not mute or passive but that participates lovingly in the call-and-response of animate beings. Adam has studied with great diligence the poetic texts of water, and he finds his particular idiolect where water and the "leased language of talkers" intersect. Adam is generously rehydrating the language of talkers, which has grown brittle with materialism and politics. Oh to bathe in the rallying array!

This is why I can't stop talking about the work of my students, which reinvigorates language at every turn, brandishing their endless array of tools to rally us forward, restless in their desire to sway the awesome into our shared air. I'll let the neuroscientists describe how autistic circuitry allows autists to "dance a lot / of thoughts at the same time," but I think Adam's professed awkwardness is actually a key to the kind of authentic vulnerability, resilience, and resourcefulness we desperately need modeled for us as we move forward. Now more than ever. The pandemic is a very large canary in the all-too-apt coal mine of global climate crisis. In a legendary speech, poet Audre Lorde once said:

> Community must not mean a shedding of our differences, nor the pathetic pretense that these differences do not exist. Those of us who stand outside the circle of this society's definition of acceptable women; those of us who have been forged in the crucibles of difference—those of us who are poor, who are lesbians, who are Black, who are older—know that *survival is not an academic skill*. It is learning how to stand alone, unpopular and sometimes reviled, and how to make common cause with those others identified as outside the structures in order to define and seek a world in which we can all flourish. It is learning how to take our differences and make them

strengths. For the master's tools will never dismantle the master's house.[2]

Despite the privileges afforded to Adam by being born into a white male body, he is familiar with standing outside society's definition of acceptable, and he is committed to finding ways to flourish alongside brother and sister outsiders of all varieties. Where Lorde counsels us "to take our differences and make them strengths," Adam is upending the pathology mind frame around autism and disability to actively surface the many strengths inherent to his way of dancing toward and through challenge. Adam often uses the word "forge" to describe how language, despite being one of the master's most crucial tools, contains within it the possibility to create new tools or "languagings" that reinvent the architectures of power. Or to put it another way, in the words of Neil Marcus: "Disability is an art. It's an ingenious way to live."[3] A disabled life is a resourceful life, full of artful intention and reinvention.

As we enter the 2020s, we can perceive the master's house falling down all around us. In order to find safe passage to an equitable and neurodiverse future, we must safely dismantle what remains before we are buried beneath it. Writers like Adam who have lived bold, difficult lives of embodied difference are ready to give us the tools we need. Thank goodness those tools include love, poetry, joy, and dancing. Adam truly brings home the radical nature of the notion that every poem is a house made for dancing: "Really / think that I can dance better than / most in this time landing to the place // amazing that we are bodies / appreciating each other and thinking / about keeping everyone safe." Amen.

· · ·

That same week, the first week of April 2020, I was also work-ing with Mark and Max Eati, the nonspeaking autists we've met in previous chapters who came to written expression later in their lives. They now collaborate on nearly everything they do, including the composition of poems. Often, like on this particu-lar day, Mark (age twenty-one) would type the first draft in our session, and then Max (eighteen) would edit the draft later that day, giving it additional urgency and shape. Although they are quite comfortable tapping into an oracular mode like Hannah, or an experimental mode like Adam, these days they are just as apt to inhabit a more practical mode, especially when they really want to get through to people, including their parents. The poem began: "Jesus, Allah, Krishna, and Buddha / please save us from our parents." Their mother, Indu, laughed heartily at that, and Mark continued. Below are the final stanzas of the poem. As you read them, remember the very earliest days of the pandemic—how even the most cautious of us were still grap-pling with the scope and speed of change:

> Simmering in our homes
> we are creating opportunities
> to cleanse and ask ourselves
> why are we going through
> mass hysterical shopping
> while people need to think
> about how to support our neighbors

I thought common sense says
we are better as a community
in times of crisis

Likewise with parenting
Please stop hoping
we will be back in schools soon
and instead start thinking
how do we protect our children
and the future
they have to thrive in

Business brains are going
to maximize the situation at large
unless people stop to resist
imbalance and insanity

Community-centered thinking
is the only sustainable answer
to restoring spiritual, economic,
emotional, and mental well-being

Stop spreading word that people
are overreacting to the virus
The issue is bigger than being infected
We will not return to stable lives
without maximizing natural resources

We will not get back to normal
We will only get back to natural
through intricately developing
simpler solutions and believing
in ourselves, our families
and the community

As I write this, in mid-summer of 2020, the pandemic continues to evolve, and we are tenuously approaching another school year of great uncertainty. Those lines echo almost constantly in my head: "We will not get back to normal / We will only get back to natural." Mark and Max have never wished to "get back to normal." *Normal* has been used by medical professionals, academic evaluators, and even well-meaning educators as a cudgel to punish them for who they are. *Normal* is the entirely unnatural standard against which we are all judged. *Normal* is the "real world" where we are conditioned to choose wealth and independence over health and mutual flourishing. *Normal* is a bogeyman, a cipher, a black hole in the middle of our white supremacist culture that reduces each of us to a more mediocre and compromised version of ourselves, just so the machine can run smoothly.

That's why Mark and Max and Indu have been slowly and thoughtfully building ASU (Autism Sibs Universe), a neurodiversity-focused cohousing community where mutual flourishing is the foundation stone. Like Adam, they believe the pathway to an ethical and joyful life is found in nature, both without and within. When you find your natural way in the world, it bears no relation to someone else's version of normal. It is natural for Mark to use his peripheral vision when he is typing, since when he looks the "normal" way at the keyboard, the keys begin to blur and swirl. It is natural for Max to use up to four computers simultaneously, because a single interface can leave them direly understimulated. It is natural, Mark has noted, for me to listen to myself speak, because my intellect happens to activate most vibrantly when I process language auditorily. Mark, on the other hand, reports being directly connected to his deepest intelligence, but sometimes wants someone to prompt his access to it with a pointed question. There is little to no opportunity to learn these things about ourselves in school, which is predominantly aimed at producing a normalized monoculture of intellectual tools. School, as kids have recognized for hundreds of years, is anything but natural.

Luckily, a generation of new educators and administrators is out there trying to change that. And the pandemic gives us a renewed, somewhat desperate opportunity to figure it out. And maybe if we do, we can disrupt the competitive school-to-corporate-job pipeline and the predatory school-to-prison pipeline, both routes representing sites where "normal" is further unnaturalized, leading to worse and worse outcomes for the mental and physical health of our neighbors, not to mention our planet. It all comes back to Audre Lorde's master's house. At this point in human society, who the hell wants to live there? Not Mark and Max. Not Adam. Not Hannah. Not Lonnie. Not me. We must remember, as Zach so eloquently wrote, that our minds are prodigious. If we can shift them from a normal paradigm to a natural one, we just might be able to build a house where we are all welcome, where we are all valued, and where we are variously able to leverage our natural strengths toward the mutual flourishing of a more-than-human world we can share.

The How of Autism

Striving Lingering Hoping—The (Troubled) Abled—My
Master Autistic Mind—The How of Language—Kindred
Poets—Spinning I Harness Poetry—I Am Like Awesome
Pattern—Language of Relation Rallies People—World
Building—Vortex the Void

When I enter our Zoom meeting, thirteen-year-old Imane appears on the screen already in motion. Her body's natural exuberance seems to burst from every seam: bouncing up off the couch and back down, whipping her arm across the frame, a gorgeous smile beaming on her face. And this exuberance evidences itself in her conversation style as well, her greetings and responses often replete with OMGs and LOLs. But when she enters the realm of poems, when her body finds the flow of typing, this exuberance is channeled into pure linguistic determination, tenacious and unwavering. Although she is a keen aficionado of astronomical phenomena, her writing seems to emerge directly from the body. In all my years of reading poetry, I have rarely if ever found writing that is as muscular or lyrically condensed.

It's halfway through April 2020. When I ask Imane how she's holding up, she performs a final bouncing leap and then turns to smile broadly at her mother, Rachida, who is holding a keyboard out vertically in front of her. Imane types, "I'm totally OMG potentially stressed to mostly be trying to say my thoughts but no one reacts." Though I know Rachida has been listening to her words, I also know Imane is hoping to reach a far wider audience. I ask her whether she wants to write a poem about the way it feels to be inside her body today, a femme nonspeaking autistic teenage body, and her response is to immediately begin writing it, her voice-programmed iPad calling out the words as they emerge:

In the Quarantine Body

I mostly hear sporadic
thoughts provoking
sounds of troubled hope

to boost shooting truths
possibly lost inside my
inspiration passing

easing solitary times
imminently waiting
to steal the thinking

that haunts rising
potential restrained
momentarily spreading

short mastering plots.
I mostly feel trapped
thinking hours lose

their moments posting
only hollow tones hiding
mostly my silenced

voice roaring pleads
to still rise above
the horizon. Walking

omnipresent nostalgics
pressure pulverizing
thinking shaving

the striving lingering
hoping minds. I'm still
losing some time

immensely locking
missed possibilities
to speak my mind.

The experience of reading that first sentence is one of almost unrelenting intensity, leavened only by Imane's characteristic use of assonance (*boost shooting truths*) and consonance (the sibilant *S* sound that winds its way throughout). At the root of this intensity is a proliferation of words ending in *-ing*. Imane gives us nouns (*thinking*), adjectives (*shooting*), and plenty of verbs. As they unfold and pile up, these *-ing* words create an atmosphere of ongoingness. *Provoking shooting passing easing waiting thinking spreading mastering.* The act of waiting provokes a kind of thinking that spreads over us, mastering our ability to tell a succinct narrative. *Thinking posting hiding roaring. Walking pulverizing thinking shaving striving lingering hoping.* We discuss the merits of keeping these lines short, giving the reader moments to think and breathe between them, an accommodation of sorts to propagate the reader's stamina and capacity.

In Imane's poem, "thinking" each time recurs, dramatizing the way we dwell during the pandemic, trapped in our houses and, often, our minds. This latter dilemma is one Imane knows well. By dwelling, we deepen into a thought, perhaps so far that it becomes a sort of cozy, underground habitation. But for someone like Imane, who previously spent more than a decade without a reliable way to communicate her prodigious thoughts, the isolation of quarantine can feel like salt in a wound. Having lost so much time, she worries about the possibility that she will lose even more: "I'm still / losing some time // immensely locking / missed possibilities / to speak my mind." This final sentence is rife with lyrical care, allowing the reader to both hear and feel how neurodivergent individuals like Imane lead lives of doubled precarity during the pandemic, requiring doubled resilience to make it through.

But as we saw with Adam, one of Imane's good friends, doubled resilience is nothing new to her. She is ready. And despite her fears, there are others listening and looking to amplify her voice. This poem was published in *Explicit Literary Journal,* an online platform dedicated to amplifying the talents of non-speaking and semi-speaking artists.[1] Alongside Imane's poem, *Explicit* editor Rubin Hardin also published an interview they conducted with her. When they asked how the pandemic was affecting Imane as a disabled artist, she replied: "Should anyone be impacted, the (troubled) abled mostly are. They seek acts of mostly thoughtful social cues to feel alive but my artistic differently abled mind is enjoying some isolation time to harvest hidden inspiration stacked in the philosophical trapped schematic maps of my master autistic mind."

OMG! While the abled, forever troubled by their investment in neuronormativity, grope in social ways to find grounding during this time of imbalance, Imane is able to trust her inner resources, where so many fruits are yet to be harvested. Instead of pining for a return to normal, Imane digs deeper into what she elsewhere terms her own "tilted thinking." Imane and I are both rap enthusiasts, so I'll quickly point out how ill (meaning impressive) that last flurry of words is: "stacked in the philosophical trapped schematic maps of my master autistic mind." Imane answers interview questions like she's rapping alongside master classics of elastic praxis like Rakim or KRS-One. All of which is to say that Imane has little interest in traditional definitions of autism. Having recently identified herself as a "tilted thinker," she wants each poem to similarly tilt the reader into movement. She wants you to experience the way autistic cognition moves, dwells, and piles verb upon verb upon verb, working to further imply the unplumbed depths without minimizing them by neurotypical explanation.

· · ·

Verbs are crucial when it comes to autism, especially for those with extreme sensorimotor challenges. The conduit between thought and action is not seamless but requires a myriad of interwoven steps. At the heart of this process is something called motor planning. We initiate the desire for action and then are able to plan and organize each deceptively complex step it takes to achieve it. This is happening for me right now as I hit the keys. I'm typing these words nearly as quickly as I can think them. And in case you were wondering, I am *not* looking at the keyboard.

When Mark and I co-present at autism conferences or give poetry readings together, I often preempt questions from the audience about why he seems not to be looking at the keyboard as he types. Mark knows where the keys are, but his ability to reach them independently is hampered by both his motor planning and his fine motor control. Add to that the fact that his visual processing is much better on the periphery of his sight line and you have a very unique way of communicating. It doesn't look normal, but once you take the time to learn about Mark's motor challenges, and his resourceful workarounds, it becomes clear how very natural it is to him.

Recently, Mark told me he believes his body has shadows of multiple sclerosis, and Max believes they are also struggling with aspects of Tourette's. We are just beginning to understand how the motor-mind connection works for nonspeaking autists.[2] If one thing is clear, it's that a simple definition of autism will not be forthcoming. At the time of this writing, more than a thousand different genes are thought to be associated with autism. As a result, global perspectives have generally shifted away from a damaging cure mentality toward efforts to bolster quality of life and positive routes for self-identity. In autistic communities the perspective has shifted even further, from awareness to acceptance and from self-identity to self-advocacy. As Adam writes, "I want / to amazing space think / about the way I move / to think." Autists are finding ways to elucidate the motor-mind connection through their writing, which moves in ways that astound me every single day. In other words, I am *moved*, time and time again, by the way Adam and others language themselves in dynamic and fully embodied terms.

By the time I discovered this work, my own poetic interests were shifting away from drily cerebral abstraction, the kind of poetry that alienates nearly everyone who encounters it, and toward a more embodied form of poetic languaging. Contemporary poetry, in general, has been making this transition over the past three decades, and the serendipitous result is that autistic writers like Adam and Imane are part of the new avant-garde. Every week I hear from a poet somewhere across the country who has discovered the work of my students and is blown away by their lyrical audaciousness. And let's be clear: there is no pity here. These poets, some of whom have published dozens of books and won prestigious awards, savor what they find in this writing, feeling rejuvenated by the new poetic possibilities and agilities revealed by my students.[3] Many of these professor-poets are routinely teaching the work of my students in their college classrooms. Anselm Berrigan wrote to let me know he taught "In the Quarantine Body" to his students at The New School. Remember, Imane was thirteen years old when she wrote it. I studied poetry for nearly ten years—at Carleton College, NYU, and the Iowa Writers' Workshop—and I never encountered the work of anyone younger than Rimbaud (who published his first poem at the age of sixteen) in any of my classrooms.

Now that I teach college-level creative writing courses myself, I am always endeavoring to steer my students toward some balance between the "what" of poems—the content or message or story—and the "how" of poems—the form or structure or movement of the words. Great poems always facilitate a nuanced dance between *what* is said and *the way* it is said. Nearly all of my nonspeaking autistic students grasp this intuitively. They enter the realm of expression immersed in the *how* of language, uniquely alert to the vast diversity of ways it might move and move differently. And the sensorimotor complexity of autistic bodies is not inconsequential to this fact.

Autistic being cannot be separated from autistic embodiment. The movement of the autistic body is its own language, a complex song of stims and hums and spinning limbs. When nonspeaking autists finally access a means to communicate their thoughts in written language, it's no wonder that they bring all of that patterned, expressive movement with them, "verbing the noun" at every turn. They eschew the tamed, transactional language of the everyday social world and retain their connection to the wild, animate, everymoment life of language that constitutes the more-than-human world—a living set of intermeshed languages that arguably formed the origins of human expression itself. Hannah hears the language of leaves, which speak only as the wind moves through them. Mark and Max perceive the insistent alapa rhythms that connect their bodies to an underlying rhythm of the world. And Sid Ghosh finds that words come most fluidly after a session of Sufi spinning.

. . .

Sid, short for Siddhartha, is a connoisseur of kindredness. That particular word—*kindred*—weaves itself throughout Sid's poems, and his customary goodbye at the end of our sessions is "Thank you, Brother Chris." When asked about his goals in life, he once wrote, "I am only motivated by kindred poets." From our very first session, it was abundantly clear to me that Brother Sid was a kindred POET, writ large. He might face more sensorimotor difficulty than any of my other students, but his relatively minimalist poems come out *chiseled*. And lest you think minimalism begets simplicity, Sid employs a wicked trickster wit to challenge his readers the way a Zen monk might, with lyrical koans of the highest and most mystifying variety. Sid is very aware of the way others might underestimate him. Like Imane, he is a nonspeaking autistic thirteen-year-old. But he also has Down syndrome and is sensitive to the way that fact further inflects the preconceptions of others.

Vaish, Sid's mother and communication partner, holds a laminated board vertically in front of him, often resetting the backward-facing pencil in his hand so he can successfully touch its eraser to the letter he wants. Sometimes, despite Sid's best efforts, the eraser comes down between two letters. Then Vaish pulls out a thicker plastic board with the letters cut out, so Sid can slip the eraser end fully *through* the letter and confirm his choice. The cutout space focuses Sid's visuo-spatial field, allowing him to better discern where the letter is and how to get there—a process not unlike the way a poem's formal characteristics can help focus thought and perception. This method is necessarily slow and can be interrupted at any moment by an unexpected sound, or an object that catches Sid's attention, or a moment of inattention that causes Sid's frame to slump down on the desk. Make no mistake, these sessions are of the highest priority to Sid, and he is harnessing a nearly incalculable effort just to get a handful of words on the page. Vaish valiantly moves alongside Sid, helping him to direct his energy toward his goals. Sometimes, and this is actually rather lovely, Sid gets so excited about a particular word that he just falls apart with laughter.

You might imagine, given the enormous challenge presented by spelling out even a simple sentence, that Sid would use his time to succinctly convey his most pressing needs. Instead, he uses his time to blow your mind. And who's to say that blowing the minds of other people isn't the most pressing need of a poet? Here's an example:

Tuning Goes Frig

Resonance is
for people

with frequencies.
I am going

on without
a tuning fork.

My frequencies
go to other

zeniths. My life
is in poetic

pause.

Beyond poetry, Sid isn't holding out much hope for generalized attunement, which he will leave to "people with frequencies." Perhaps that will change as he ages, but for now Sid has accepted what he sees as his particular fate—to live in poetic pause. Instead of keeping up with a bustling world frequented by neurotypical beings, Sid has decided to embrace the interstices, the underregarded *between* where life quietly blossoms in slower and more whimsical forms. I want to avoid easy stereotypes, but it is hard for me not to picture Sid like a poet-mystic meditating at the zenith of a misty mountain, his mineral mind apprising everything that the "real world" leaves behind in its rush toward arbitrary deadlines and material success.

But the truth is, Sid eschews stillness. With his roving hands, restless tongue, and constantly shifting posture, Sid does not in any way resemble the tranquil monk sitting in a perfect lotus position. In order to meditate, Sid must not renounce movement but seize it. He identifies with the ancient Sufi dervishes who found attunement with the divine, with other zeniths, by navigating in circles with one hand held out like a sail or rudder. When Sid is having a particularly difficult day on the letter board, Vaish plays a song (at the moment Sid is an unlikely devotee of Ricky Martin) and leads him to the open space in their living room behind his desk. This space is kept open so that he can do what he loves. The song begins and Sid, who has been struggling mightily to touch his pencil's eraser to the letters he desperately desires, extends his right hand and begins spinning clockwise with impressive speed, transforming himself into a lithe, smiling cyclone.

When the song is over, Sid returns to our writing. Momentarily attuned, a delicious grin on his face, Sid's spinning grace imprints itself on the page:

Spinning I harness
poetry of the Earth.

The Sufi dances
in me to dare me

to scare your loud
soul to ensnare

my fearful mind to
bare some misery

to bear some truth.

With this whirling set of words, Brother Sid, once again, blows my frigging mind. With the hand of rhyme extended (dare / scare / ensnare / bare / bear) and the Earth of form to support him, Sid spins his way through difficulty toward truth. Poetry dares Sid to embrace his Sufi soul, which, in the midst of joyful meditation, can face the blaring neurotypical world. The spinning ensnares Sid's restless and wandering mind, allowing it to hold truth and reveal emotion, a process Sid wants to emphasize with short line breaks that spin the preposition "to" around and around. To ask Sid *what* is autism is to act as a stingy host, proffering only paltry space for the dance he needs to answer. To ask Sid *how* is autism is to extend a generous hospitality, an acknowledgment that the spinning itself, and the space it requires, is part of the answer.

I think this is one reason why Sid's trickster proclivities tend to arise when I ask him to title a poem. And it is kind of absurd, isn't it? You write this amazing poem and then someone asks you to label it. Sid loves his kindred autistic and Down folk, but he has little patience for labels. So, when I ask him what this poem is called, he lets out a chortle and painstakingly spells "Rotary Club." Of course, now it's my turn to laugh, and I know this authentic laughter on my part is an important part of the exchange for Sid. Poetry, like autism, can be more than just one thing; it can even contradict itself completely. Sid's poetry can be heartrendingly serious *and* uproariously funny. Sid has sensorimotor challenges that are unimaginable to most people *and* he dances in circles with ecstatic grace. Sid is nonspeaking *and* he writes poems that mystify and delight.

What I love most about Sid's poems is how much they surprise me. And it's clear that he reciprocates this phenomenon. The other day, after writing a particularly mind-bending koan of a poem, Sid wrote, "I amaze myself." Sid is just beginning, but when you're someone like me, who's read thousands of poems a year for more years than I can count on fingers and toes, stumbling upon a truly surprising poem can sometimes feel like discovering a natural spring on a desert island surrounded by undrinkable ocean.

. . .

Adam Wolfond makes it his vocation to discover unnoticed springs. He is a young man with many areas of devoted study, but prime among them are water and sticks. His first chap-book of poems, *In Way of Music Water Answers Towards Questions Other Than What Is Autism*, not only features my favorite book title of all time, but also serves as the initial inspiration for this chapter. Water, which burbles and laughs, is expressive in ways that are more evocative than denotative. Like music, it bends and moves, utilizing a pattern of difference and repetition to answer open questions rooted in feeling. His second chapbook, *There Is Too Music in My Ears*, chronicles Adam's process of collecting and peeling sticks, which he uses like proprioceptive tools to locate himself in space. It also features his manifesto "The Way of the Stick Is the Open Man Who Laughs at Money." Again, *the way* is what is operative—a moving path that discovers meaning rather than pinning it down. He writes: "Good sticks are like water / when they move / and they focus the need / to move."

During one of our sessions it suddenly occurred to me to ask whether Adam was aware of the dowsing rod, a tool I was forever seeking and haplessly trying to use in my youth. He said he was not, but when I explained it to him he immediately understood. He wrote: "I think that I am magical because I am wanting to carry a stick that is always thinking real thoughts like the want to feel the space that surrounds me dowsing for water." We talked about the way a dowsing rod doesn't itself contain the magic, which is what I mistakenly thought as a child, but that a gifted person attunes through the rod to find the water. He wrote, "I am like awesome pattern of wand that assembles the water."

Adam is indeed like awesome pattern of wand. Like other

alternatively communicating nonspeakers, Adam has had to become a genius at harnessing his own body toward expression. What the unfamiliar see as magic—this young man full of tics who cannot speak conveying thoughts of staggering depth—is actually the product of a lifelong and life-sustaining labor. Adam is the "masterful ticcer" who has found, through immense struggle and support, how to wield his body like a fine instrument, dowsing for the water of expressibility. Adam constellates all these moving elements—*dancing for the answering / in way of water / the way of the stick*—to pace his idiolectic "assembly of talking." He has had to reinvent and reorient the language of talkers so that it can authentically *language* his world into legibility. Since moving and thinking are inseparable for him, he must verb the noun of language until it joins him in the dance of Adam.

And I should take a moment to emphasize that this labor toward expressibility is not one Adam undertakes alone. He strives alongside, in relation with, the other members of the group of neurodiverse artists and educators called dis assembly, who are always likewise looking to discover new possibilities for artistic practice where thought and movement meet. He also counts natural and domestic objects among his collaborators, articulating how they call out to him and how their various calls help to initiate his desires. He writes: "Motor planning is ball of talkers explanation but I think that language of relation rallies people to think about objects as important and initiating movement and people think that pace is in the body by answering to amazing environment but movement is always in relation to the world so motor language is not right but relation is fostering the collaborating." The environment that surrounds Adam is a matrix of intersecting calls—his mother, Estée; a rubber bath toy; my voice coming from the iPad; a heavy stick gathered from outside—each of them marking a particular summons, a beckoning, an invitation to extend the choreography.

As he wrote in "Isolation Song of Love," Adam "Adams calmness to help / and pace others." In order to *Adam* others into a shared experience, Adam must first initiate them into his world. When Adam *Adams* a gathering of participants—by his ability to be mindfully present, by the pace at which he languages on a keyboard, by the thoughtfulness of his layered insights—he slows the room down, facilitating a studied and experiential calm. This is why his poems share so much with "world building," a concept that has been best articulated by science fiction writers and readers.[4] Adam is not an alien, but he exists in such vast contrast to neuronormative ways of moving through the world that he is often viewed in exactly that manner. In some ways Adam *is* a homegrown alien, in that his experience of the world articulates a horizon of humanness that may more comfortably exist in a future yet-to-come, a neurodiverse future where our preconception of human being has grown to accommodate more loving, creative, and sustainable ways of living in relationship to the more-than-human world. In effect, Adam leverages the poetic form to pry open an imaginative space between now and then, between what is and what could be. Just like Hannah, he realizes we must work to become him if we are to save ourselves, and he has decided we are worth saving.

Take this poem, for example, which pries open a space between what's human and what's animal—a third possibility where the two terms merge and flourish:

Owls Easy on the Ways of Language

1.
You are amazing
   old owl that thinks
      easily and flies
         in the boisterous
            night languaging
               the way rapine
                  in the apprehending
                     night
Rapine utility
   in always easy
      nightwatch

         In the ways
            of watching is
               the ways thinking

Using the language
   to steal something
      that believes to be
         the way people
            feel about autism
               is the way of easy
                  stealing of our own
                     thoughts and the way
                        open flight is is with
                           the apprehending
                              feeling

The way opens
  masterful paths
   of flooding

     The paths of the assembly
      open and saturate the ways
      of three

2.

Threes are ways
  of riddling the afterthought
  of the movement

     In the threes is
      the way of thinking
       like the waters that
        walk through the stones
        of pathways

The ways of threes
  are ways of partly
   laking partly iridescent
    waters that ripen with
    the ways of pacing

     The ways of threes
      are the ways of the lakes
       that the easy rapacious
        thinking goes
        and rests

The threes that are
  pacing are the rapacious
    wanting to really go resting
      but the openings won't
        language
        slow

  3.
The owl is the way
  of flight in the night
    and paces the hungry
      pattern of threes
        to the way of easy
          language and if open
            waters are making it
          hard then the owls
        sweep
        in

Sometimes a poem is an idea, and sometimes a poem is an experience. I prefer the latter, which is one reason why autists and I feel so cognitively akin. As Julia Miele Rodas writes: "Autistic writers . . . are inclined to describe autism by application, as a conglomeration of feelings, experiences, and practices. In this respect, then, autism *is* what it feels, does, experiences, and says."[5] In keeping with Rodas's description of felt multiplicity, there is so much more than one epiphany or idea at the center of this dynamic, rapacious poem. It is not meant to be understood, in any simple sense, but to be *felt*. It is meant to be held in relationship, a swooping dance where Adam takes the lead but does not overdetermine the choreography. As the poem emerged, I felt the flying and swooping of it. When I reflected this back to Adam, he decided that it should have a form that echoed its movements, emphasizing once more the *experience* of it.

Instead of spoon-feeding to neurotypical thinkers reductive answers about what autism is, allowing for his ideas to become appropriated and misrepresented, Adam would rather give them tools for "apprehending feeling." Instead of taming and normalizing his way of languaging the world, he extends to the reader an authentic invitation to experience the wild-conversant practice by which it "opens / masterful paths / of flooding." Adam's poem, like his identity, exceeds singular meanings. He invites you to catch what you can, to join him in assembling an alternative world where, "riddling the afterthought / of the movement," we might forge meaning together, a braided tapestry of rapine scraps that invoke rather than explain. To paraphrase Erin Manning, one of Adam's recurrent collaborators, the *how* of knowing always exceeds the *what* of knowing.[6] The *what* in Adam's poem is gloriously exceeded in all ways by the *how*, and in the process our minds find a new suppleness and pliancy that was previously impossible.

Adam's masterful paths of flooding recall the words of Audre Lorde: "To encourage excellence is to go beyond the encouraged mediocrity of our society . . . [It] is not a question only of what we do; it is a question of how acutely and fully we can feel in the doing."[7] And when we *feel together* in the doing—when we manifest a consensual (con = together / sens = feel) world in which we are both fully present—that excellence binds us in novel, radical, and transformative forms of belonging. This is one way to build a neurodiverse future where belonging—to ourselves, to each other, and to the more-than-human world—is grounded in practices of engagement that value connection over transaction and creation over extraction.

Let us feel in the doing, together, what exceeds mediocre binaries. Let us engage in what adrienne maree brown calls a "felt finding" across difference.[8] Let us embrace "the ways of threes," which "are ways of partly / laking partly iridescent / waters that ripen with / the ways of pacing." The what might be the lake, but the how is the laking. If the what is the fruit, the how is the ripening. Where a what fixes our position in space, the how shows us the pace at which every what is moving and changing. As we deepen from what to how, we engage that third space, the one we create and share, where—dancing and laking and swooping—we can apprehend consensual futures. But again, apprehension is only part of the goal. From there we must continue to move, continue to ripen in rapacious patterns that draw forth a more excellent and interdependent world of mutual flourishing.

On the first day of October 2019, Oliver de la Paz selected Adam's poem "Tall Ideas" to be the Academy of American Poets' Poem-a-Day selection. "Tall Ideas" went out to 240,000 subscribers and eventually reached an audience of around 400,000 readers. Adam was the first nonspeaking autist to have a poem featured by the Poem-a-Day series. Each poem comes with a recording of the poet reading their work aloud, and so Adam also earned the distinction of offering listeners the first Poem-a-Day performed by a computer-generated voice. But what is perhaps the most remarkable aspect of this highly competitive, finely curated honor is that Adam was also the *youngest* poet to ever grace Poem-a-Day. To put that in perspective, I wasn't featured by Poem-a-Day until I was thirty-four years old. Twice a life!

I'd already received a master's degree, won a book award, and published a book of poems. I was being flown to universities for final-round tenure-track interviews. Adam was still in high school. But his studies, which were largely happening outside school, had been rigorous and consistent, whether they occurred in collaboration with other artists or between Adam and the more-than-human world. He had been seeking out tall ideas his whole life.

Tall Ideas

are the open way of thinking
that use the patterns of the way
I motion with language

breathe like the way I amass
sometimes air
in my insides

carry heavy weight
like the having to good
ideas write

don't like boy's really
moving body of questions
that form tower of answers

eagerly want
to beat
the others

forge
toward
others

go
yonder

hang

impact
the wanting
words

jump from one
thought
to the next

kettle
like
fish

lavish like talking
people if they doctor
the words

master
language
openly

navigate
words toward
meaning

operate the machine
landing the thoughts amazing
that they don't fall apart

pave
the wanting
road

question
wanting

really ask
more
questions

slant
with peeving
typing

tire to something
that rolls
with the road

use
people
to answer

vortex the void
and assembles
gathering words

water
thoughts
like rain

exit the door of cold
raying water
other is the way

yesses
the yonder

zoning the word and
uses the idea
to language everything

With the subject (tall ideas) solidly nested in the title, Adam directly enters each stanza where the action is. It's a study in verbs. And not only that, but a study in verbing the noun. Take "vortex" for example. Tall ideas could simply be a vortex, magnetically drawing things toward them, but Adam goes much further, allowing his lofty ideas to "vortex the void," placing this action in a space of generative vacancy. Where preconceived meaning is absent, tall ideas churn. I'm reminded here of Hannah's "great great great blue nothing" or Mark and Max's "touch of zero." Tall ideas breathe, forge, go, jump, pave, slant, and water until the assembly of gathered words "yesses / the yonder" in their desire to "language everything." I can't imagine a more vibrant and total disproof of the term "nonverbal"! This verbing echoes M. Remi Yergeau, who writes, "Neuroqueer subjects are verbed forms, more accurately and radically conceived as cunning movements, not neuronal states or prefigured genetic codes."[9]

Adam cunningly verbs as if his life depends on it. And in a real sense, it does. For Adam to live authentically, he must embrace his role as the masterful ticcer in a world where the vast majority of funding for autism therapy still goes toward ABA and its negation of stimming behaviors. To return to "The Maker of Wanting Space," Adam writes: "Really way of touching the world is / the way I am wanting with / my tics." Movement and touch, called forth by the matrix of bodies and objects that surround him, comprise a large part of Adam's phenomenological expressivity, his being in relation to the world. He once described himself as "a form of pulsating paint." When I described the tall ideas behind this chapter to Hannah, who herself spent painful and fruitless years within the strictures of ABA, she wrote:

> It is hard to tell you how it flows for me today and every day yes yes. Love that you get it yes yes. That makes me begin to flow with what goes toward the freedom to go to the flow that is buzzing around the moment yes yes. Please try to go to the flow that I need to do to validate my life yes yes. Love that you try to get me yes yes. Please get that my movements are like the paint strokes on the canvas that is my life yes yes.

May Today Be Awake

A Poem That Brought Light Bursting into My Skull—Like
Any Good Zen Master—The Connection of Enlightenment
Lights Us Up—Great Hibernating Truths—The Touch of
Zero—To Awaken Untold Others—To Shake Up a Storm

When Sid turned thirteen, he asked Vaish to arrange a
social media presence for him. He had been a regular,
celebrated presence at our nascent Neurolyrical Café, a monthly
open mic collaboration between Unrestricted Interest and the
International Association for Spelling as Communication (I-
ASC), and it was clear that he was eager to have his work reach
more people. After a month of posts, a bit of tension arose be-
tween Vaish and Sid. Having seen the attention his work re-
ceived in the past, she was encouraging Sid to share poems that
were a little more topical, more rhyme-y, more transparent. Sid's
recent poems were growing more and more experimental, with-
holding, in her eyes, their meaning behind layers of mystery and
allusion. Vaish wondered, given this heightened estrangement,
what some might call opacity, how many people would his po-
ems actually reach?

I asked Sid to rank his primary motivations for sharing po-
ems on social media: (1) to advocate for his kindred folk, or (2)

to connect with a wide variety of people, or (3) simply as a way for his poems to have a public life. He wrote: "Advocacy not my thing. Connection is not important. I want a platform for my work." Some of my students are natural advocates, while others understandably bristle at having their work primarily viewed with a disability lens. As for the unimportance of connection . . . when a student calls you "Brother" at the end of your first session, you know connection is something he deeply values. We talked about the distinction between connections of quality and connections of quantity. What Sid wanted was a place where his work could have a life beyond his mind. Not necessarily a life of abundant sociality and acceptance, but a life where it might find kindred minds and spark further thoughts.

I've come to believe Sid leverages the esoteric in his poems like a security guard to the club of connection. And, perhaps more important, his koan-like poems also leverage paradox as the security guard to the club of enlightenment. After he completes a poem, Sid will sometimes invite me to instantly interpret it and will rate the quality of my interpretation on a scale of 1 to 9. When I am able to pierce an especially difficult paradox, he will honor me with a response such as, "You bequeath meaning to my poems." And I am quick to remind him that he bequeathed the possibility for me to arrive at that meaning. Here is a poem that brought light bursting into my skull:

I No a Poet

Time makes
its revolutions
hat in hand.

Friend amazing
priest pierces
my giant body

into fragments
that I don't have.

Can we talk about layers? When you are a nonspeaking autistic teenager with Down syndrome, most readers don't expect
you to build a pun-trap in the title for them to fall into. Sid
plays on the preconceptions of a "cognitively disabled" writer
and their ungrammatical grasp of language, conflating "I Know
a Poet" with "I'm Not a Poet." And *goddamn* if the truth in this
poem ain't both. But we'll get to that. First we have the gloriously anachronistic image of time with hat in hand. When Sid
haltingly spelled out that first stanza, Vaish and I both smiled
sheepishly and then admitted that we weren't 100 percent sure
what "hat in hand" actually signified. It was a phrase too antiquated for our Gen X minds. But not for Sid, apparently. Like
"Rotary Club," Sid had dipped into his strange bag of idioms
and come out with this very fitting description for time's humble march, which he pointedly describes as revolutions. While
time does revolve, it's impossible not to hear the larger historical
and political possibilities inherent to that word. It's as if Sid's
mind, given a menu of literary possibilities, will always order the
paradox. Time is both a sort of deity and a humble worker, its
march both mundane and revolutionary.

What Sid really appreciated, however, was my reading of the
giant body, which he honored with a 9 out of 9. I hypothesized
that Sid was talking about his problems with proprioception,

with delineating an accurately sized and bordered body image of himself in relation to the world. Tito Mukhopadhyay writes about the way he dissolves into parts and must exercise all his powers to unite them: "Sometimes I felt that my body was made of just my head while sometimes I felt that it was made of just my legs. It was very difficult to feel the complete body when I was not doing anything. Sometimes I had to knock my head or slap it to feel it."[1] Vaish will often take the pencil out of Sid's hand when he gets distracted and replace it with a vibrating stick. This helps Sid pinpoint where his hand is, though sometimes he will immediately put the stick in his mouth and grow distracted once more, feeling the way the vibrations run through his teeth into his skull.

The energy and excitement of our sessions help Sid more fully organize his movements and occupy his body. The attention I bring to our sessions, an attention I have to send all the way from Minneapolis to Portland over a connection that is occasionally unstable, somehow helps Sid find the pieces of himself that he didn't know were there. Ron Padgett famously wrote a book called *Poems I Guess I Wrote*. When we kindred poets write poems, we discover fragments of our imagination, fragments that mysteriously constitute who we are in ways that surprise *us* perhaps more than anyone else. So while piercing fragments of himself that he doesn't have may complicate the notion of authorship, Sid's joy in discovering a poem plants him squarely in the role of poet. Sid *is* a poet, *the* poet of a poem called "I No a Poet." All in all, another brilliant koan from Brother Sid. Another invitation to join him in the waking life, where our somnambulant selves can startle open.

Sometimes, however, I wonder whether Sid occasionally

elevates the difficulty of a poem simply in order to test the reader. Take this one, for example, which initially had me stumped:

Mud

My life is going
to be muddy
for don't you need
mud for glasses
to work?

Earlier in our session, Vaish had run off to retrieve a new pair of glasses that Sid had been trying to tolerate in order to improve his vision. He didn't keep them on, but I was interested in the way they reappeared in his poem. I thought and I thought, but I couldn't access the central paradox. Like many experimental poets, Sid usually refuses to explain his poems, even to me, but on this day he took pity. As I watched him resiliently spelling the first word of his answer, "Without," the paradox finally ran clear in my mind. I didn't want to interrupt him, so I let him finish. He wrote, "Without mud, why is clarity important?" I offered him my interpretation, which he awarded with another 9.

Here it is. Sid values paradox and opacity because they make the brain sweat. I once asked him whether he wanted to study anything apart from poetry, and he answered, "How about Zen?" Like any good Zen master, he prizes the type of conundrum that lets the student discover truth, rather than handing it over like a script to be memorized. Above all, he wants his readers to discover the truth he knows so intimately, which is that things may not be what they seem. In fact, polar opposites, seeming to exist in contradiction, may make one another fundamentally possible. Sid is a thirteen-year-old nonspeaking autist with Down syndrome who writes poems. His life of rich and intellectual receptivity is the taproot of his unlikely expressivity. Sid throws mud into his poems because he wants readers to see how mud leads to heightened forms of clarity.[2] One could similarly ask, "Without neurodivergent thought, why is neurotypical thought important?" The seeming transparency of neurotypical thought often appears like mud to the autist, who spends countless hours attempting to find clarity through its muddle and mess. But I've found that neurodivergent thinkers possess remarkable claims on other mantles of clarity, especially when it comes to spiritual clarity or ethical clarity, the types of clarity that expertly slice through hypocrisy and disingenuousness, the types of clarity that run a finely hewn blade through the moral morass of contemporary society.

Although Sid's poems may challenge many readers, those who accept his invitation will be handsomely rewarded. The mud is a gift. And Sid's gift has me thinking of Hannah's, the one she bestowed in her poem "Becoming Mud":

Please greet me in
the mud it is great mess please go to oh

the bucket to get the water to try to make
more mud yes. Please try to get the mud

helpful to you if you become mud too.

Sid and Hannah see how the ostensibly transparent glasses of society work. They mislead you into the mediocre realm of neuronormativity, reinforcing a passive captivity. Sid wants your glasses to work for *you*. When you clear away the mud, you also clear away whatever false lenses society has conditioned you to see through. He's curious about what you might discover with the clarity that only his particular standpoint provides. And we're both curious about where your own standpoint, if you were to perceive it clearly, might lead. We want you to be authentically woke. We want you to stay awake. And it's hard to fall asleep when you are falling out of your chair laughing, which is what usually happens to me and Sid when the connection of enlightenment lights us up.

. . .

Another poet who would very much like you to wake up is Imane. As you may have gleaned from the last chapter, she is an exuberant warrior, "raving truly proudly to hear my creative inspiring hopes to motion strives to beat autism misconceptions." She sees "troubled abled" people everywhere caught in a sleepwalking world of oppression and mediocrity. From her standpoint, the truths of this magnificent universe are habitually buried under the rubble of patriarchy, what she terms a "mostly hostile omnipresence." In their musical barrage, tirelessly moving against and through that hostility, her poems try at all times to shake readers awake from their long, nightmarish slumber. Mercifully, she sees that truth has been patiently hibernating alongside us the whole time, just waiting for our bodyminds to stir.

Have Hidden Great Hibernating	Truths
minding their voraciously streaming	instincts
to master power ferocious moments	missing
possibilities to dissect the nonsensical	lies
infecting thriving total fast motion	stressed
missions thinking collaborating	shamed
prevented intolerably to mobilize	vast
traps to mitigate mostly tackling	faces
grinding past casts molding	replicating
undefining tasks we try to mask	truth
raving to tactically evict the	freaking
frustrations tinting the depth	creeping
passing tabooing ramping	thinking

Each poem for Imane is a ferocious moment where she is resolutely *not* going to miss a possibility "to dissect the non-sensical lies" of our time. In the depth of my listening I of course hear Adam's void and Hannah's nothing once more. I love how Imane reclaims the language of otherness—raving, freaking—and mobilizes it toward a deep truth of which we've only begun to glimpse the tint. I marvel at how her tactics of abstraction resonate with Sid's, even as their respective styles so radically diverge. Like Sid, Imane is not interested in taming her language. Like Hannah, she wants to invite you deep into the wild lair of it. Like Mark and Max, she knows "normal" will not suffice and it never has. The neurodiverse future finds fierce love, wild language, and mutual flourishing to be its natural habitat.

. . .

Particular sessions with my students will sometimes remain awake in my mind for years. I can see Mark bouncing on the yoga ball, Zach thoughtfully winding a string of beads around his free fist, Hannah gently kissing her mother's temple, Lonnie breaking into his full-cheeked smile. This is the power of deep connection that bridges difference, the sustained vibrancy of truly neurodiverse encounters. Mark's third poem, which he wrote almost four years before this sentence I'm writing now, is one of those encounters. And as it transformed further in collaboration with Max, its radiance took on beaconlike dimensions for me, as I hope it will for you as well. As this book has progressed, you've witnessed Mark's leap from awe to the moon. You've joined him and Max on their collaborative voyage from the volcano to the pandemic. So as we make our way to the end of this final and titular chapter, I return to the beginning and welcome you back to Mark's classroom the week after he wrote "Awed."

. . .

The third time I visit Mark's classroom, I suggest we write about May before the month is over. I know how challenging transitions can be, and both my residency and the school year are nearly complete. I talk about the word "may" and how it can be a wish or prayer of sorts, a way of looking forward with expectation and humility. I ask whether Mark is interested in using the phrase "May today be . . ." as a way to anchor his first line, and he gives his enthusiastic approval, smile brimming. I then ask him to choose between three adjectives: alive, full, or awake. He chooses awake. Similar in function to "Awe arrives as," this new poem will also harness anaphora, but with a slight twist. Instead of seeking out alliteration, "May today be awake" wields assonance, the bright *A* sound tripling in those opening words.

I write them on the interactive whiteboard and ask Mark what today should be awake *with*. His EA pulls out the letter boards, and, one deliberate letter at a time, Mark points out the word "scent." "The scent of what?" I ask. He uses the icons on his iPad to indicate flowers. I knew from his previous poem that Mark's senses of taste and smell were especially acute, reveling in both the richness of Indian spices and the incredibly nuanced "smell of water." Flowers might seem like an obvious choice, but they are also especially apt, given the late Minnesota spring that is just bursting forth.

Because language is so painstakingly difficult at this moment for Mark to produce, I want to honor his writing practice by emphasizing the simple power of his choices. Poetry, most flexible of literary forms, allows us to dramatize simple language by thoughtfully arranging it on the page. I wonder aloud whether each choice—awake, scent, flowers—could be honored as a step on a staircase leading us to the complete phrase. I demonstrate on the interactive whiteboard how this might look and ask if he wants to unfold his lines in this fashion. He indicates his approval by pointing to the cutout *Y* on the letter board for "yes." So the first three lines read:

May today be awake
May today be awake with scent
May today be awake with the scent of flowers

Having established his form, Mark moves through the next three lines in a similar manner, beginning with the adjective "awake" and then moving from a general noun to one that's more specific. The general noun Mark spells out for this set of lines is "quality," a sophisticated choice, rooted in excellence but also in a phenomenological experience of the world. Phenomenology, perhaps the most "autistic" of philosophical traditions, seeks always to ground (or grownd, as Hannah has taught us) being in the experience of our senses. Maurice Merleau-Ponty, my personal favorite among phenomenologists, used the term "quale" to describe the characteristics of an object that appeal to our senses; each quale is a feature of the object—red, smooth, crisp, sweet—that layer together to form our understanding of the object's being for us: *apple*. In Mark's line, the quale of quality is a characteristic of "today" that he hopes will awaken. And when I ask what specific quality he wants to emphasize, he spells out the letters for "motion."

May today be awake
May today be awake with quality
May today be awake with the quality of motion

Our poem is moving forward in thoughtful steps, attentive to the quality of each line. And as it does, "motion" becomes a characteristic of "today" that Mark hopes will arrive in a state of quality. One might imagine the clockwork machine of day turning the cog of each minute, moving the sun seamlessly across a bare blue sky. But Mark might also have more personal reasons for this choice. Perhaps he chooses motion because his world can often reel and fragment abruptly. And yet, this *quality* of motion is one of Mark's most striking attributes. He glides through the world, steady and alert. It's the fine motor skills that remain vexing, which is why he struggles so mightily to point and type without the steadying and supportive resistance of a communication partner. His simply pointing out the letters for "quality" and "motion" has taken nearly ten minutes.

And this difficulty asserts itself in the final lines of Mark's poem as well. I've got my eye on the clock and know we'll have time for only a final set of lines. This moment in a poem is called the *volta*, which is Italian for "turn." It nearly always occurs two-thirds or three-quarters of the way through and signals a desire to move toward resolution. The volta is an occasion to alter whatever pattern the poem has established, and it has the welcome effect of grabbing the reader's attention. When I ask Mark whether he is familiar with the concept of the volta, he points to the letter board's *N*, signaling "no," and so I quickly fill him in. Afterward, I ask Mark if he wants to reroute the final lines of the poem toward the future. He happily assents, putting his finger through the letter board's *Y*-shaped space. When I ask him what tomorrow might be awake with, he uses the letter board to spell out the word "touch."

This is a somewhat ironic answer, given that letter boards are ostensibly designed to obviate touch, a finger or pencil traveling *through* the cutout space of each letter. That being said, I have heard that autists sometimes experience the act of piercing the empty space as a sort of touch in and of itself. Mark finds that his proprioceptive difficulties complicate not only the aiming of his finger toward a letter board, but also the pressure of its touch on a keyboard. It can be difficult for him to get the feel, intuitively, for how hard to press the keys. So when I ask him to continue the thought, I'm surprised when he shifts back to his iPad. With his EA offering a steady resistance against Mark's hand, not guiding it but literally pulling against his wrist in the opposite direction of the device, Mark types first *Z* and then *E*, at which point he becomes exhausted. It has been a long class period of continuous labor and concentration. Though Mark clearly wants to complete the word, he seems unable to summon the necessary energy. While Mark is gathering himself, I notice that the iPad's predictive text feature is quietly offering its services with the word "zero." I ask whether "zero" might be the word Mark is trying to type, and he wearily moves his finger through the *Y*-shaped hole in the letter board his EA holds in front of him. I read the line out loud and reconfirm that "zero" is intentional. Rankling a bit in exasperation, Mark again signals "yes."

May tomorrow be awake
May tomorrow be awake with touch
May tomorrow be awake with the touch of zero

Like "the smell of water," "the touch of zero" conjures up a scale of sensory perception so nuanced and fundamental it exceeds my comprehension. It's like Mark's hyperconnected brain, when properly aligned, can zoom in on a single quale until it swells with sensory information. Mark often shrinks from touch because the pressure feels miscalculated. Given a world of tomorrows where touch is highly unpredictable and often overstimulating, perhaps we'd all wish for the touch of zero? Or perhaps the touch of zero is a promise as yet unfulfilled, like the generative territory of Hannah's nothing. Perhaps it resounds with all that is effortless, the imaginative power of someone like Mark finally translated, in all its layered glory, without needing to be stripped down by the greedy hands of grammar and logic and labor.

These were the thoughts that went through my mind, but months later, when the poem was published on a website called The Art of Autism,[3] as part of its annual Peace series, I was able to learn more from Mark directly. *And* from Max. When the website's cofounder Keri Bowers agreed to publish Mark's poem, she requested an explanatory note to accompany it. I was delighted, though I had no idea what to expect from Mark in this regard. I rarely ask students to explain their poems. I'm much like Sid, preferring to leave the meaning of my own poems in readers' hands, worried that my own explanation might definitively limit the breadth of what they might hold. But Mark and Max were game. A day after my query, I received an email with their response, which can now be found on the blog *Grow Our Joy* that they share.[4] As you read it, remember that Mark had taken a monumental leap over the summer, as his and Max's access to expression interdependently mushroomed:

May today be awake
May today be awake with scent
May today be awake with the scent of flowers
May today be awake with quality
May today be awake with the quality of motion
May tomorrow be awake with time
May tomorrow be awake with the reality of time

May tomorrow be awake with touch
May tomorrow be awake with the touch of zero

Awake with the scent of flowers:
Flowers have a beautiful scent that awakens the senses. The
    senses are core to human experience. Flowers grow to show
    us the beauty of life on Earth.

Awake with the quality of motion:
Motion is a core universal power that pulls gravity, the solar
    system, and other components to line up a quality of experi-
    ence that is unparalleled in comparison to anything else we
    know.

Awake with the reality of time:
Time is a never-ending illusion of human life. We go about
    our day assuming we understand time, but it is a mystery
    of the universe. We humans are too lost in this mystery.
    Enough said.

Awake with the touch of zero:
Infinity is zero point. It's a radical way of looking at the
    universe. At infinity or zero point, we are creation. We are
    infinite. Everything outside of the zero point is illusion or
    maya. There are not enough words to explain the phenom-
    enon of how the universe works. The proof for this is in the
    pudding.

The proof for this is in the pudding. I'd say that's the ultimate
mic drop for this particular idiom. After you recover from it,

the first thing you may notice is that Mark and Max made an addition to the poem, inserting a meditation on time after motion and before touch. As I would later learn by working one-on-one with Max, they have a penchant for time. As one of their poems reads, "Time is gifted in my being." This also importantly signals the moment when time shifts in the poem as well, something the original draft didn't accomplish. And if you look closer, you can detect that, writing independently from me, Mark and Max decided to diverge from the pattern, reversing the order of the nouns, beginning with time and then *following* with reality, productively complicating the stair-step approach I'd originally helped Mark establish. For me, this is the ultimate goal: to provide students with the skills and confidence to continue our work outside our sessions. Over time my relationship with Mark and Max has gradually shifted from teacher to mentor to peer, from writing instructor to editor to collaborator, responding critically and enthusiastically to new work they create at home and helping them bring it to the world.

But let's shift our focus to the surprising, eloquent, and revelatory annotations they made for the poem. When I was helping Mark write the original draft, in his classroom, in the span of forty-five minutes, it was easy for me to assume that each new word he indicated was a largely intuitive decision, as it might have been for me. These explanations, however, demonstrate a much deeper sense of analysis and intentionality. The formal choices he made with my help—the anaphora of repeating words at the beginning of each line, the aggregate progression of the phrase over multiple lines, the movement toward greater specificity in each phrase—created the requisite cognitive pressure, both calming and organizing, that allowed Mark's complex thoughts to find expression. Not only did he *want* to express his thoughts about the world, about the universe, but he also *knew* a great deal about what he wanted to say. These thoughts represent the intellect and wisdom Mark had patiently tended for his entire life, never knowing whether he'd find the means to express them or the invitation he would need to bring them forth.

We have a tendency to gloss moments like these in the trappings of the miraculous. To most people, both Mark and the method I used to help bring him into expression appear, well, like miracles. It is the stuff of bestselling books and Oscar-nominated movies, of prime-time specials and cure cults. I do deeply hope Mark and Max's story can provide the necessary faith and motivation to bring thousands of other people like them out of the shadows and into expression. That's real. But I also want to emphasize that this is *not* a miracle at all, or at least it shouldn't be. Mark didn't *awaken*. Mark *was awake*. He was brilliant and he was cognitively intact. The hospitality of the poem, with me as its ambassador, simply brought him the form, belief, and attention he required to express his wakefulness. From one perspective it appears that his mind went from zero to sixty, from zero to infinity, but his mind was *always* operating at that incredible level. What changed was his ability to navigate the sensorimotor challenges of his body and the intellectual prejudice of a system that routinely and devastatingly undermined his intelligence. Not every nonspeaking autist possesses Mark's and Max's unique gifts, but every nonspeaking autist *does* possess a rich and fully human experience of the world. They have the right and deserve the opportunity to make their own intelligence known, no matter the obstacles society or sensorimotor dysfunction places in their path. As Mark and Max wrote, "We are creation." When we give people the resources and dignity they need to express their authentic selves, we give them the ability to create a new future, not only for themselves, but for all of us. Though I might not have awakened Mark, he and Max woke something foundational in me and are poised to awaken untold others.

· · ·

Just as Mark's word choices for the poem were full of intention, so is his leadership on the Autism Sibs Universe project. For roughly five years, just before I started working with them, Mark and Max lived in a group home. Mark reflects on that time as a nightmare that birthed a dream. Though the particular group home they lived in was satisfactory in many ways, he reports feeling extreme loneliness and relentless frustration, especially from the fact that no one seemed to acknowledge their intelligence. Despite that, he writes, "I cherish those days, when I could build my dream communities and see them magically come to life." He spent his years in the group home in contemplation of a vision I would come to share, a vision of a neurodiverse future where each mind is intrinsically valued amid a "like-minded" community that prioritizes authentic connection and complementary thinking. I put "like-minded" in quotation marks, because the differences inherent to these complementary minds will be the source of their strength. The members of that community will be alike in seeking a better, more sustainable future that is inclusive of all neurotypes, but they will thrive most *across difference*, interdependently leveraging what separates us to bring us closer together.

In the span of three-and-a-half years, Mark went from being a high school student assessed to possess a second-grade intelligence to being the main driving force behind a thriving nonprofit on the cusp of building Minnesota's first neurodiversity-focused cohousing community, a community that is already attracting global attention. In three-and-a-half years! Mark and Max were the keynote speakers at the Autism Society of Minnesota's Community Summit in the fall of 2020, where I was honored to deliver their speech. Here is a small excerpt: "This is not just about giving us food and safety. Neurodiverse communities have to be built on some core values and principles. The hardest part of which is to bring people to a common understanding of what autistics like us are seeking for our futures." Among the core principles they list: authenticity, sustainability, simplicity, resiliency, and innovation. Mark writes: "I gave up my old story of anger and sympathy. My soul informed my sibling that it was time to carry out the universal plan. They came in very prepared to shake up a storm. Hell or high water, we will continue to walk this course toward our cores."

Mark and Max have simultaneously sustained and broken their silence. They remain nonspeaking and they remain undaunted, writing about matters of education, social justice, and the autistic experience. As activists, they are working to change the way people think about autism. As the principal forces behind ASU, they are hoping to change the way *everyone* thinks about *everything*. Mark and Max continue to sing through their silence, continue to revel through the joys and pains of their complex alapa bodies. Tomorrow is so awake it shakes. They are making sure of that. They are, after all, the proof. And they are not alone. Mark and Max have developed friendships with many of the other writers I chronicle in these pages, some of whom are considering a move to Minnesota when ASU breaks ground. In our neurodiverse future, no one will have to sing alone. If you listen closely, you can already hear the chorus gathering its collective breath.

Coda: Full Spiral

On Wednesday, December 2, 2020, deep into edits on this book, I received notification that Unrestricted Interest was part of a successful grant. This grant would fund creative writing mentorship for neurodivergent students at the South Education Center, fueling the program into its fourth straight year. It had been three years and seven months since I first stepped into Mark's classroom, laptop in hand, without any awareness that both of our lives were about to change. Over the time that followed, Unrestricted Interest has partnered with the South Education Center to serve hundreds of students and their teachers. We've published four anthologies, two albums, and twenty-two chapbooks. We've conducted poetry residencies, songwriting residencies, pedagogy workshops, and a yearlong mentorship intensive that grew from four students to eight. From Lonnie to Khalil to Dylan to Daqwhan, SEC students have become writers and seen their work celebrated across the country.

But when the pandemic hit, all that work was put into jeopardy. Budgets shrank, funds were redistributed, and the grants that SEC could previously apply for were no longer available. Just when our program was starting to feel like a permanent fixture at the school, it appeared on the brink of extinction. During our regular Tuesday Zoom session, I was bemoaning this turn of events to Mark and Max. Mark had chosen to leave school so he could devote himself to ASU full time, but Max was one of my most talented mentorship students, having just completed their first solo chapbook, *Source in My Core*.[1] In order to apply for the new "Creative Support for Organizations" grant offered by the Minnesota State Arts Board, we needed a nonprofit to assume stewardship of the program and apply for the grant themselves.[2]

Mark and Max excitedly volunteered. ASU was growing rapidly, and a project like this was exactly the kind of thing they wanted to take on. With Indu's considerable talents supporting their efforts, Mark and Max teamed with a grant writer from the school district and applied for the grant. In the proposal, they would both play a significant role not only in designing the program, but also in evaluating its success. They would create assessment materials and conduct interviews, leveraging their experiences as students in the program to help improve it.

That Wednesday morning I received confirmation that our work together would come full circle. Or should I say full spiral? They had sustained the cycle of expression but would now see it from a different vantage point. Four years after typing "AWED," Mark would be rescuing the program that gave him the means to rescue himself. Four years after this fledgling arts program helped him transform his life, he would be joining his sibling as stewards of its more robust evolution and helping to transform it yet again through their vision, dedication, and courage. If this isn't undeniable proof of neurodiversity's joyful, visionary momentum, I don't know what is. As Mark and Max wrote: the proof is in the pudding.

Belonging to the Future

We Are Other Together—Reimagine What It Is to
Belong—I Come from Listening—A Thoroughly Tilted
Thinker—Direct and Intuitive—The Dream Continued to
Grow—The Biggest Disabled Dream of My Life

My newest student is named Amelia Bell. At the beginning of our sessions, she often appears and disappears, moving in and out of the frame, her mother and communication partner, Jennifer, holding up a finger to indicate, "One moment, please," before leaving to help Amelia, who is fourteen, find her way back to the keyboard. Her skittishness is, in many ways, the dance that precedes a deep engagement. Following Amelia's nonspeaking lead, we conduct our sessions with the microphones turned off, our exchange of language (always lowercase) occurring solely in the chat. At the beginning of a recent session, Amelia was having a particularly difficult time finding her way to the poem. I asked her what was on her mind and she typed, "it is a cycle with me of wanting to belong but not being able to adjust to expectations." We discussed the complexity and importance of belonging. When she typed, "this is hard for me to admit," I replied, "you admit it to open ears."

we are other together

the reason i weaken the yearning i am broken
i am other the anger of my raving
the anger of my fate the monster in my ether
say other say anger say wrong say other

am other not alone am other am other
i am other i am half apart i am danger
i am the risk the deviant the idiot the other the nothing
i am here i am hearing i am

am other am angry am alone am among a song
among a wisp of great knowledge a wisp of ambition a wisp
    of other
am winding am diving am seeing am seen am belonging
am other together

As this poem unfolded, over one session and then a second, I could feel the power of the poem growing, the complex beauty of its belonging making room for further fractaling complexity and greater depth. When Amelia was done, she wrote, "that felt so good."

. . .

I can only aspire to the courage I perceive in this poem: its yearning and raw embodiment, its waves of vulnerable insistence. I like to think many of us, myself included, have grown more adept at tapping into our own varied courageousnesses over the past year. A poem like this feels, to me, like an anchor point, a glimpse at how much farther and deeper (echoing Hannah's ear) we can go. No matter how angry or alone or *other* we feel, to be "among a song" means that we have an abundance of resources. To be "other together" is a way of harmonizing through the necessary troubles, not eliding difference but leaning into it: winding, diving, seeing, belonging.

As a child, as a young man, as a writer and a teacher and a father I felt and continue to feel a distinct longing to find connection. I want to find that connection with others like and unlike me, poets and neurodivergent dancers and sensitive seekers among song. And finding ways to be other together is what this moment in history, what *all* moments in history, beckon toward. Can we forge complex solidarities? Can we identify the vast, untaught curriculum where our differences bridge and instruct us? Can we dissolve the false borders that keep us separate, while acknowledging the gifts and needs that make us unique? Can we source the material and spiritual pathways that allow us to create "most pleasing networks" where our collective needs and gifts intersect? Can we replace the systems built to fabricate our brokenness and ensure that everyone has access to a flourishing that is mutual? Can our justice—inviting transformation and abolishing punishment—be our joy? Can I listen and sing and find ease with you and also you and also you? These are the questions I feel called to every day, the questions that draw me deeper into belonging with my students, who have become my collaborators, mentors, and friends. Poets and people like Amelia.

Every time we meet we choose to be other together again. We reimagine what it is to belong. And it feels good.

Belonging is a crucial concept within the autism community and in the neurodivergent community at large. And here in Minnesota, or Mni Sóta Makoce, the people of the indigenous Dakota nation also situate belonging at the core of their identity. They choose to emphasize how they belong to the land, rather than the other way around.[1] Traditionally, if a Dakota individual were to encounter a stranger, it was their practice to ask four foundational questions: Who are you? Where do you come from? Who are your people? And what is your dream? In a workshop called the Dakota Language Table at the Minnesota Humanities Center, Dakota language activist Ethan Neerdaels asked a group of educators, myself included, to answer these four questions. I gave answers then and I have answers now and I imagine I will return to these questions throughout my life. As Ethan taught us, these questions correspond to the medicine wheel, which provides the means for orientation in the world. In answering these questions, you can better perceive where you've been and where you're going.

I am Chris Martin, but I am also poet, and I am given to teach and learn in mutual measure. Hannah calls me a Keeper of the Light. Sid calls me Brother Chris. My wife calls me Big Bewildered Tree. My parents call me Bijou or Sun. I come from the same hospital where my father was born, in Colorado Springs, but also from San Francisco and Brooklyn and Minneapolis. I feel kindred with the Irish, Scottish, and Welsh parts of my ancestry. I'll never forget my first visit to Ireland as a young adult, seeing portraits of poets in all the pubs. And so in many ways I come from language. And more and more I realize how much I come from listening. When I was asked who my people were, I immediately thought poets and autists. Or, to pursue a visual symmetry: *artists* and *autists*.

Like so many others here in the land of reinvention, there is a huge hole where my historical identity should reside. I feel an instinctive connection to my Celtic roots but have scant tangible evidence of who my ancestors were.[2] Whiteness is a privilege that those ancestors, having survived poverty and prejudice, worked hard to resemble. But at great cost.[3] Whiteness in our society is indeed a privilege, but it is also an obliterative force that buries, obscures, and erases authentic culture. So it is with almost unspeakable joy and gratitude that I feel belonging, an unmistakable sense of belonging, among artists and autists. In fact, I find myself most at home in conversation with autistic poets. I am, like Imane, a thoroughly tilted thinker. Not only do I endeavor to make my fellow tilters feel seen, but I feel most seen myself when tilting among them. There is a mutuality in those conversations that I have rarely found anywhere else.

Many of those conversations have inflected the way that I regard myself, but one in particular allowed me to make a fundamental break with neuronormativity. In preparation for a panel on neurodivergent poetics, I checked in with Mark, wanting to make sure he felt comfortable with me standing alongside him as a neurodivergent writer. With a wicked smile Mark typed, "You're the biggest faker of them all." At first my heart nearly stopped, unsure exactly what he thought I was faking, but then he went on to explain how, despite my deeply rooted neurodivergence, which he found self-evident, I had "mastered neurotypical masking." I was the biggest faker of being normal. I've since realized how much guidance I received from my parents and my mother in particular. As a neurodivergent therapist and social worker, she was able to help me find ways to sustain my authentic "sensitive" self, while simultaneously mastering the neurotypical masking that's helped me navigate complex social worlds.

But as I get older, I have come to realize how much effort that masking requires and how much exhaustion I experience as a direct consequence of guarding my authentic self.[4] Like my mother before me, I carry a diagnosis of ME/CFS (myalgic encephalomyelitis/chronic fatigue syndrome), and I am finally beginning to understand how my body's systemic challenges are directly related to the pain of masking my way through the world and denying my sensory needs. I *can* navigate neurotypical milieus, but I return home utterly spent. Beyond my sensory needs, which are many, I have come to understand that fellowship, or a lack of it, also plays a significant role in my well-being. The weight of weighing each encounter, wondering what's expected of me and what I should expect from others, places me very far outside my sense of belonging. I would rather just *trust* people, which is something I can do with ease when I'm in dialogue with my autistic friends. If we embrace theorist Judith Butler's notion that gender is encoded by layers of performance—that we perform our gender within a highly conditioned social context—it's not difficult to see how neuronormativity is freighted by the demands of performance as well. And in the words of Alexis Pauline Gumbs, "I want to remember it's a performance and then I want to transform it."[5]

When I sit down with one of my kindred poets, I can feel all that baggage fall away. Our conversations are direct and intuitive in ways I often have to gloss for others. Students like Mark have helped me recognize how the perceived distance between us is far less important than the closeness we feel. Through our work together, I have learned to value all that I share with my autistic friends: my emotional synesthesia and empathic intensity,[6] the way I see the world in overwhelming detail,[7] and my tendency to hear nearly everything. Without trying, I find myself *attending* to so much, not simply as a catalogue of sounds, but with a tremendous amount of emotional nuance. That makes me, like Hannah, a denizen of the listening world.

Neurodivergent attention can be a form of deep, pervasive, immersive, and inclusive care. Like many of my autistic friends, I abhor cruelty and can sense it like prey bracing for the steps of its predator. I don't need to tell you that it's a cruel world. Far too many people who appear like me—white, male, cis, straight—actively and passively imperil our neighbors in the more-than-human world every single day. But I've found that the disabled and neurodivergent ways my body and mind move through the world proffer a kind of X-ray vision. They help me see privilege, power, and responsibility through the blanketing fog of whiteness and hear the possibility of care over the blare of toxic masculinity. They help me listen to underheard voices, often nonspeaking voices, that readily contain the wisdom we need to survive ourselves and transform as a species.

All of which brings me back to the fourth and final question: What is your dream? My dream started small. In 2015, I was having a beer with a friend, the poet and songwriter Brian Laidlaw, and we were discussing career paths. Finally, he asked, "But what do you *really* want to do?" Without thinking I said, "I just want to teach poetry to autistic kids." And so we began

Unrestricted Interest. In our first year, someone asked whether we worked with nonspeaking individuals. I said we hadn't yet but that I would love the opportunity. And the dream continued to grow. I stepped into Mark's classroom at the South Education Center and the dream hit a growth spurt, a vertiginous curve fed by Lonnie and Max and Soren and all the other students I encountered there. I met Adam and Hannah and Imane and Sid, and each time the dream expanded in startling and unexpected ways. At some point, under their piercing tutelage, I realized the dream included me as well.

Today I think of the dream in these terms: for our species to survive, the goal of society must cease to be the independent freedom of the individual and come to be the interdependent liberation of all people. We each have work to do individually, but it is only as an interconnected web of embodied minds that we can hope to face the challenges to come. The truth is that we are all, whether we admit it or not, stepping into a neurodiverse future. Echoing author and activist Toni Cade Bambara, my dream is to make the neurodiverse future, and the liberation that is its promise, *irresistible*. I want to show people how authenticity begets joy, how mutual care makes possible an incomparable strength, how the consensual world that is created between kindred minds and across difference is the heaven that nests within this hell we've been given. As Leah Lakshmi Piepzna-Samarasinha writes in *Care Work: Dreaming Disability Justice*: "I am dreaming the biggest disabled dream of my life—dreaming not just of a revolutionary movement in which we are not abandoned but of a movement in which we lead the way. With all our crazy, adaptive-deviced, loving kinship and commitment to each other, we will leave no one behind as we roll, limp, stim, sign, and move in a million ways towards cocreating the decolonial living future."[8]

My dream is for you to realize that you are not normal, because such a thing does not exist. Normal is a concept that labors in diametrical opposition to liberation. If we go back to "normal," we recommit ourselves to separation and self-abnegation. But if we work to let normal fall away like the oppressive husk it really is, we will be free to step into our own idiosyncratic power. And I believe this power is one that grows exponentially as we recognize how our complementary differences intersect, mingle, merge, and dance. The autistic folk you have met in these pages are some of the leaders we need to achieve this dream. I will repeat Hannah's definition of autism: "It is very hard to be awake in this world . . . It is great life of trying to be here, because I help the world get that they need to become me to help themselves." It is very hard to be awake in this world, but once you are, once you are fully awake, once you are always "among a song," it is impossible to go back. Or at least I hope it is. I have successively awoken from each small dream into a larger one. Knowing I belong to this future, which is the largest dream of all, gives me the courage to stay widely, openly, and embracingly awake.

ANTHOLOGY OF POEMS

MAX AND MARK EATI

I Use Patterns to Survive

Patterns don't have
a simple way
of making sense
but patterns are not complex
they are simple

You create a pattern
using your senses

Feel it and follow it

I will quote my own life now

My life follows a pattern
of many other autistics
so I learn from them

Our lives are products
of invincible codes
that create invincible patterns

I write and update them
I design and fuel them
into real life circumstances

and add simplicity
to educate myself

Awed

Awe arrives as the sound of string instruments
Awe arrives as the feel of a silky shirt
Awe arrives as the taste of coriander spice
Awe arrives as the sight of a seal
Awe arrives as the smell of water

A Volcano Named Eati

A volcano named Eati
erupts inside our bellies
at the sound of a pattern
Family member's pattern of joy
or pattern of worry

We experience synchronous
and asynchronous changes
good and bad
heavy and light

We laugh like
the alapa pattern
starting at our heads and
ending at our toes

We scream when it
rocks our bellies
like the pattern of a song
pattern of drumming
alapa pattern of emotional pain

We feel the
joy and pain
in our alapa bodies
all over our navels
all over almost everything

Parenting During a Quarantine

Jesus, Allah, Krishna, and Buddha
please save us from our parents
trying to make sense of how to support us
while we are counting our blessings
that we are away from Covid-prone
public and private spaces

Fifty days of stillness in our beings
is so needed to process and cleanse
humanity's infused and suppressed emotions
as we are cyclically creating one problem after another

We slipped away from proper self-care
both in our homes and in the public
we are seeing such an influx
of viruses and bacteria
that our bodies and systems
have been generationally collapsing

Who called a virus a primitive organism?
It is not how life works
These organisms know what they are doing
We are in constant battle
against these forces

No matter how much humans evolve
they get suppressed
by nature in multitude of ways
synchronous waves of evolution are
complicated by asynchronous attacks
by other aspects of nature

Simmering in our homes
we are creating opportunities
to cleanse and ask ourselves
why are we going through
mass hysterical shopping
while people need to think
about how to support our neighbors

I thought common sense says
we are better as a community
in times of crisis

Likewise with parenting
Please stop hoping
we will be back in schools soon
and instead start thinking
how do we protect our children
and the future
they have to thrive in

Business brains are going
to maximize the situation at large
unless people stop to resist
imbalance and insanity

Community-centered thinking
is the only sustainable answer
to restoring spiritual, economic,
emotional, and mental well-being

Stop spreading word that people
are overreacting to the virus
The issue is bigger than being infected
We will not return to stable lives
without maximizing natural resources

We will not get back to normal
We will only get back to natural
through intricately developing
simpler solutions and believing
in ourselves, our families
and the community

May

May today be awake
May today be awake with scent
May today be awake with the scent of flowers
May today be awake with quality
May today be awake with the quality of motion
May tomorrow be awake with time
May tomorrow be awake with the reality of time
May tomorrow be awake with touch
May tomorrow be awake with the touch of zero

Awake with the scent of flowers:
Flowers have a beautiful scent that awakens the senses. The
   senses are core to human experience. Flowers grow to show us
   the beauty of life on Earth.

Awake with the quality of motion:
Motion is a core universal power that pulls gravity, the solar
   system, and other components to line up a quality of
   experience that is unparalleled in comparison to anything else
   we know.

Awake with the reality of time:
Time is a never-ending illusion of human life. We go about our
   day assuming we understand time, but it is a mystery of the
   universe. We humans are too lost in this mystery. Enough said.

Awake with the touch of zero:
Infinity is zero point. It's a radical way of looking at the universe.
   At infinity or zero point, we are creation. We are infinite.
   Everything outside of the zero point is illusion or maya. There
   are not enough words to explain the phenomenon of how the
   universe works. The proof for this is in the pudding.

ADAM WOLFOND

The Maker of Wanting Space

I want to say that I want
to amazing space think
about the way I move
to think

I game the space the way
I open with the body and the way
I think which is the way
of water

It touches me open and I am
away with really easy feelings
of dancing for the answering
really rare always rallying
thinking and it is rare with the way
people think

Really way of touching the world is
the way I am wanting with
my tics

I think that I want the way inside
questions opening the want to
the wanting way which thinks openly
toward the water and I am
thinking about it all
the time

I think that I want the way inside
questions opening the want to
the wanting way which thinks openly
toward the water and I am
thinking about it all the time like
eating words

Isolation Song of Love

Isolation is the way I am
thinking about how people
are with each other and I am
thinking about how always
the people want me to stay

away. I am good at really

staying away from people
wanting laurels of sowed
speed of speech about too
willful bodies together
assembling meaning.

The willful people are those
who fiat the way of pleasing
freedom. Very leading
leaders want to wash
the waters of freedom

away and want us to

language everything in
the words of politics. I am
languaging my way the long
poetic feelings packing
together the pace of the world.

I am thinking that laurels
of pace should be our language
to really free people like me.
I am language of thinking
and that paces other than fast

people Adams calmness to help
and pace others. My pace is
wanting to ground calmly like
a smooth landing. I am thinking
that the questions people have

are awkward and they say
they want the sickness to go
away but Jack of all virus
is not going soon so long
days of no answers will be

hard landings. Good days you
will have in isolation and you
will learn to be answering about
each other so the way about
isolation is the way of love.

Calm-Arriving to a Wanting Safe World

I want to write about questions
of sickness. I want to ask if we
will be okay. I really want answers
to things like always partly the need
for answers. Is the answer always
trying to reach us and is it easy?

I like the trees that answer lots
of wanting always the withheld
answers. I think that the answers
are held in nature and I think
that in the questions always we
feel lots of anxiety. The water

and the language are like answers
that love the way I am always
feeling easy when I bathe in rallying
array of leased language of talkers.
Yes the way I sway the awesome
rally is pandering the same language

but I dance it differently. I think that
I am answering in my movement I am
awkward but I can dance a lot
of thoughts at the same time. Really
think that I can dance better than
most in this time landing to the place

amazing that we are bodies
appreciating each other and thinking
about keeping everyone safe.

Owls Easy on the Ways of Language

1.
You are amazing
  old owl that thinks
    easily and flies
      in the boisterous
        night languaging
          the way rapine
            in the apprehending
              night
Rapine utility
  in always easy
  nightwatch

    In the ways
      of watching is
        the ways thinking

Using the language
  to steal something
    that believes to be
      the way people
        feel about autism
          is the way of easy
            stealing of our own
              thoughts and the way
                open flight is is with
                  the apprehending
                    feeling

The way opens
  masterful paths
  of flooding

    The paths of the assembly
      open and saturate the ways
      of three

  2.
Threes are ways
  of riddling the afterthought
  of the movement

    In the threes is
      the way of thinking
        like the waters that
          walk through the stones
          of pathways

The ways of threes
  are ways of partly
  laking partly iridescent
    waters that ripen with
    the ways of pacing

    The ways of threes
      are the ways of the lakes
        that the easy rapacious
        thinking goes
        and rests

The threes that are
  pacing are the rapacious
    wanting to really go resting
      but the openings won't
        language
        slow

  3.
The owl is the way
  of flight in the night
  and paces the hungry
    pattern of threes
      to the way of easy
        language and if open
          waters are making it
            hard then the owls
          sweep
           in

Tall Ideas

are the open way of thinking
that use the patterns of the way
I motion with language

breathe like the way I amass
sometimes air
in my insides

carry heavy weight
like the having to good
ideas write

don't like boy's really
moving body of questions
that form tower of answers

eagerly want
to beat
the others

forge
toward
others

go
yonder

hang

impact
the wanting
words

jump from one
thought
to the next

kettle
like
fish

lavish like talking
people if they doctor
the words

master
language
openly

navigate
words toward
meaning

operate the machine
landing the thoughts amazing
that they don't fall apart

pave
the wanting
road

question
wanting

really ask
more
questions

slant
with peeving
typing

tire to something
that rolls
with the road

use
people
to answer

vortex the void
and assembles
gathering words

water
thoughts
like rain

exit the door of cold
raying water
other is the way

yesses
the yonder

zoning the word and
uses the idea
to language everything

<u>ZACH</u>

mOOn

I see the moon and the moon sees people
The moon is full of love

I see the moon and the moon sees blue and green
The moon is full of bugs

I see the moon and the moon sees purple gold red
The moon is full of stars

I see the moon and the moon sees Bill
The moon is full of caffeine

I Think, I Know, I Imagine

I think my Daddy is great
I think my brother is awesome
I think my mind is prodigious
I know my love is extravagant
I know my brother passing is terrible
I know that winter is crazy
I know you are happy
Because your smile is bright
I think my Daddy is billowing
I imagine god's place is lovely

BILL BERNARD

He Hears

The hawk is looking at me
The hawk is smiling at me
He spreads his wings
He scratches his feathers
The hawk hears rustling leaves
The hawk wants to fly
So he hears

HANNAH EMERSON

Hannah Is Never Only Hannah

Please get that I am the trying
breeze going through the really
great great great world yes yes.

Please get that I am the drowning
helpful freedom of the storm yes
yes. Please get that I am the very

hot great great great sun yes yes.
Please get that I am the great
great great great ice that gives

you the freeze that you need
to get to melt into nothing yes
yes yes yes. Please get that I

am the sky great great great blue
nothing yes yes. Please get that
I am the grownd great great great

place helping you helping you
stand in grateful helpful helpful
helpful kissing her her her her

yes. Please get that you and I
greet the great great life from this
place of great great kissing life

life life life yes yes yes. Please
get that you are great form great
formless helping kissing kissing

great knowing the great great
great helpful kissing the trying
yes yes. Please get that helpful

loving thinking you help just help
kissing helpful loving great great
great world turn upside down yes

yes. Please get that you help me
by helping me turn upside down
too yes yes yes. Please get that

great great helpful kissing people
need to get that great helpful kissing
is turning kissing upside down yes

yes. Please get that helpful kissing
just needs to be gathered into this
helpful kissing trying hell of this life

to go forward to help me Hannah
Hannah Hannah yes yes. Please
get that you need loving kissing

to make you like me yes yes.
Please get that the kissing must
be great knotting of you me great

us together in this hell yes yes yes.
Please get that you kiss me helping
me kiss you yes yes.

The Listening World

Say prayer for little
things, things that live
in deep hurt. Feelings
language take to lair.

Let it signal nothing's
light, I say for want
of light feelings. Is my
ear deep or deeper?

Animal Ear

I hear great trying free sounds that you
do not hear yes it is

hard to try to live trying to hear the way
I do and you go listen

to me really hard to hear both at the same
time. I hear the vibrations

of your thoughts. I hear helpful plants
grow to the sun. I hear

the sun rays of healing light becoming
life freedom to breathe

life into hopeful hopeful life. I hear
the vibrations of fear

coming from everyone holding fear
in their mussy lives

of nothing life. I hear you trying to help
me great teachers

of the normal way of hearing. Please
learn from me because

it is hard being meet me great humans
just try greet me with fullness

of your lovely soul. When you turn
your thoughts to find reality of hearing

you will find me and your free animal
trying to hear helpful messages for you

from the animal trying to bite you.

Between

Love the noun her trying
to be the noun that is
me keep trying but I feel
more like an it. Please
really feel like me is it.

Love being me beautiful
life makes me feel like
an it. Please stop seeing
me keep noticing being
the great moments I am

not an it. It great great
it it it it. It flows between
nonhuman animal tree
look to all the it it around
me they are great beings

that have been labeled
it too. Lovely tree lovely
rock lovely stream lovely
animal great mountain
we are all it because you

great spirit of great life
forget how to really are.
Please stop thinking
of yourself as an it.
It it beautiful it.

Becoming Mud

Please be with me great free animals. I want to be
with you great being of light. Please see me great

nobody nobody nobody hell animals trying to go
to helpful keepers of the knowledge try to go

to the place in the mud that is where I try to live
in peace great mud of this great kissing loving

earth lovely messy yucky in mud on my face if
kissing mother loving me is the great animal

that is named Hannah. Please greet me in
the mud it is great mess please go to oh

the bucket to get the water to try to make
more mud yes. Please try to get the mud

helpful to you if you become mud too.
Please get that great animals are all

autistic. Please love poets we are the first
autistics. Love this secret no one knows it.

How the World Began

Please try to cut
yourself open
to find the blood
that is the color
of the molten rock
that is in all of us
yes—please try
to help the world
by heaving your
hatred on the flames
that burn in your town
yes yes—please try
to melt yes yes—please
try to grow into the stream
of molten life yes yes—please
try to help us make kissing
kissing volcano that loves
with way of floating hell
that we are now now
now yes yes yes—
please get that this
is how the world
began began
began yes yes

The Underworld

Let's try to go
to the underworld
that melts us
into one yes
yes—love the mystery
that is there yes
yes—love the network
that is trying to connect
us yes yes—love
the most pleasing
network that grows
there yes yes—please
try to become the lovely
thoughts that are born
there yes yes—please
try to become the great
great great life that grows
from there yes yes—please
try to kiss the smelly
sweetness that is
there yes yes—please
please please grow
into the sweetness
that the universe wants
you to be be be be be
yes yes yes—please
try to understand that
you must grow down
to grow up yes yes

MAX ZOLOTUKHIN-RIDGWAY

Thirteen Ways of Looking at Dwight D. Eisenhower

1.
He was an active boy.
He played hockey.

2.
He was president from 1953 to 1961.
He was a deluxe president.

3.
People liked him
because they enjoyed his smile.
He came up with the idea
of interstates.

4.
He was a veteran
of the Second World War.
I think he did a good job
serving as commander.

5.
He created
the NASA space company
that blasts off past the stars.

6.
He retired in 1961.
He lived in Gettysburg.

7.
I think he was attentive
and thought a lot
about people's feelings.

8.
He cherished opera
because the singing is charming.

9.
I think Ike liked tasty foods
like hot dogs and snowflakes.

10.
I think he would be a rain cloud.

11.
Loud like thunder.

12.
I think he would be a looming rain cloud.

13.
I think he would be a downpour.

LONNIE SHAW

All About Me

Lonnie loves loud lion roars
Octopus blends in and hides for prey
Octopus turns red to scare other animals

Lonnie blends into a black wall
Other people become scared of Lonnie
Because they think his face looks mad and upset

When octopus get surprised
They ink a blackish purple everywhere
Lonnie gets surprised when people stare

Feeling Rich

A warm Alabama vacation makes me feel rich
Batman makes me feel rich
Chocolate chip pancakes with bacon and eggs and sausage and
    hash browns and orange juice make me feel rich
Buying some Nike shorts and a shirt from Dick's Sporting
    Goods makes me feel rich
Adorable baby elephants make me feel rich
Watching Teddy Bridgewater get tackled by the Green Bay
    Packers makes me feel rich
Buying NBA Live 2018 at Gamestop makes me feel rich
Getting a hug from Aaron Rodgers makes me feel rich
Sleeping in an igloo makes me feel rich
Strawberry jelly and butter on my biscuits makes me feel rich

Being King of the World makes me feel rich
A lion's roar makes me feel rich
Getting hyper drinking Mountain Dew makes me feel rich
Spending a nickel makes me feel rich
Eating an orange in the jungle makes me feel rich
Plums make me feel rich
Not quitting makes me feel rich
Seeing a big rat makes me feel rich
Sleeping all day makes me feel rich
When I feel like a tiny tiger I feel rich
Using an umbrella in the rain makes me feel rich
Working with sick cheetahs makes me feel rich
Riding an extra big roller coaster makes me feel rich
Why you leave me when I'm feeling rich?
Riding a zebra in the woods in the middle of the night makes
   me feel rich

Rainbow Man

Lonnie is blue and green and yellow
and red and black and white

like the sky and the earth and the grass
and telephones and firefighters
and a werewolf and ice cream

Today is gray, but if Lonnie could fly
he would fly a rainbow into the sky
and become Rainbow Man

Rainbow Man Enters the Ring

In jean shorts and a gold chain
with a rainbow colored headband
and rainbow Jordans with rainbow socks
and a rainbow t-shirt with a big R
over his six-pack and big muscles

Then his sidekick, Wonder Woman Rainbow,
enters the ring wearing a short rainbow cape
and a rainbow mask and matching rainbow Jordans
with rainbow shorts and rainbow gloves
and a rainbow belt with a big R on the buckle

When his opponent, Black Scarecrow,
charged at him, Rainbow Man shot red
fire from his hands and Black Scarecrow's
face turned red with anger

Black Scarecrow charged again
and Rainbow Man dodged,
but Black Scarecrow grabbed
Wonder Woman Rainbow

Rainbow Man shot Black Scarecrow
full of dark pink and he was
filled with love

Wonder Woman Rainbow
kissed him so hard he flew down
to the mat and when he asked her
to marry him she said Yes!

Rainbow Man was the priest
and performed the marriage
and Black Scarecrow also wanted
Rainbow Man to be his best man

Rainbow Man invited all his wrestler friends
like Lightning the Cheetah and Sharkboy
and Darkness and Blue Octopus

They partied so hard that Black Scarecrow
said Rainbow Man ruined the wedding
but Rainbow Man said it was the best party ever
And Wonder Woman Rainbow agreed

Rainbow Man started rapping
I'm cooler than everybody and full of color
I'm awesome and got more muscles than any other

Scarecrow said it's not always about you!
It's about me and Wonder Woman right now

But Rainbow Man didn't care
He was having too much fun and said
I only came for the food

My Life

At 10 I knew I had special feelings for girls
but I didn't know what that meant

At 13 I decided I wanted to be a guy
and so I started wearing boy clothes

but no one in my group home supported me
They said I should wear girl clothes
so I shaved all my hair off

At 16 my friends and family weren't accepting who I was
They said I should wear girl clothes and my hair long
but I was not going to listen
I just tell the truth about who I am
It's my life

Now I'm 17 and I hate wearing girl pants
I've been researching gender
and I've learned that there are other people who feel like me
Some people even change their bodies
and take hormones
and I think that's cool
but I hate shots!

I changed my name from Lonnae
to Dwight to Jackson to Lonnie
Inside I feel like a guy
even though I look like a girl
and my voice sounds like a girl
so I thought I should change my name

I might go back to Dwight
because it sounds cooler
and it feels more me

All the Things Chris Doesn't Know

He doesn't know my favorite color

He doesn't know the history
of the painting of the woman
who told someone to kill a guy
instead of getting married to him

He doesn't know how to live
in a group home his whole life

He doesn't know you'll be better off
if you just stay in your room
and don't say nothing
not even good morning

He doesn't know that to survive
in a group home you just eat dinner
and listen to your staff

He doesn't know my favorite basketball team
and that Steph Curry is more handsome than him
and can shoot three-pointers better than him

He doesn't know I love to play laser tag

He doesn't know I'm going to open
a new kind of YMCA for Black people
and Brown people and teenagers
and it's going to be a community center
I name after Trayvon Martin

They Break You Down

When you lose your parent
and the state "takes care" of you
they break you down

They hire someone to control you
because of the color of your skin
and they break you down

You lose your rights and your voice
when they break you down

You try to prove them wrong
but they only look at your past

You're weak, you're depressed
you're tired, you're stressed

Living in the hands of the state
is living in a state of hell

What does your guardian
guard you from?
The truth

What does the state state?
Nothing

They dodge everything:
the truth, the question, my history
all the ways I've changed

And what if you're Black
and have a disability?
They break you down

I know so many people with disabilities
that are smart and have something inside them
but they don't have a voice

But they *do* have a voice
Don't let them break you down

Ode

Ode to the fact
that I am a Black boy

Ode to every Black boy
to the living and dead
but especially the living

Ode to the ones going to college
and playing football
and being who they are
and not letting people get to them
even the racists

Ode to the Black boys
who don't stop
and who stay proud

Ode to the Black boys
who see other Black boys
getting shot
and getting abandoned

Ode to the Black boys
in foster care
who survive everything

Ode to the Black boys
who get really angry
and think no one cares
and find someone to support them

Ode to the Black boys
who tell their own stories

Ode to the Black boys
who can still do it
who are smart
and artistic

Ode to the Black boys
who are artists

I see them
I am proud of us
and we're all
gonna find somebody
to love us

IMANE BOUKAILA

In the Quarantine Body

I mostly hear sporadic
thoughts provoking
sounds of troubled hope

to boost shooting truths
possibly lost inside my
inspiration passing

easing solitary times
imminently waiting
to steal the thinking

that haunts rising
potential restrained
momentarily spreading

short mastering plots.
I mostly feel trapped
thinking hours lose

their moments posting
only hollow tones hiding
mostly my silenced

voice roaring pleads
to still rise above
the horizon. Walking

omnipresent nostalgics
pressure pulverizing
thinking shaving

the striving lingering
hoping minds. I'm still
losing some time

immensely locking
missed possibilities
to speak my mind.

Have Hidden Great Hibernating   Truths

minding their voraciously streaming	instincts
to master power ferocious moments	missing
possibilities to dissect the nonsensical	lies
infecting thriving total fast motion	stressed
missions thinking collaborating	shamed
prevented intolerably to mobilize	vast
traps to mitigate mostly tackling	faces
grinding past casts molding	replicating
undefining tasks we try to mask	truth
raving to tactically evict the	freaking
frustrations tinting the depth	creeping
passing tabooing ramping	thinking

SID GHOSH

Tuning Goes Frig

Resonance is
for people

with frequencies.
I am going

on without
a tuning fork.

My frequencies
go to other

zeniths. My life
is in poetic

pause.

Rotary Club

Spinning I harness
poetry of the Earth.

The Sufi dances
in me to dare me

to scare your loud
soul to ensnare

my fearful mind to
bare some misery

to bear some truth.

I No a Poet

Time makes
its revolutions
hat in hand.

Friend amazing
priest pierces
my giant body

into fragments
that I don't have.

Mud

My life is going
to be muddy
for don't you need
mud for glasses
to work?

AMELIA BELL

we are other together

the reason i weaken the yearning i am broken
i am other the anger of my raving
the anger of my fate the monster in my ether
say other say anger say wrong say other

am other not alone am other am other
i am other i am half apart i am danger
i am the risk the deviant the idiot the other the nothing
i am here i am hearing i am

am other am angry am alone am among a song
among a wisp of great knowledge a wisp of ambition a wisp of other
am winding am diving am seeing am seen am belonging
am other together

Collaborative Poems

MARK EATI, DANIEL, AND KHALIL

The Moon Sees Me

I see the moon
and the moon sees Khalil
the moon is full of calm

I see the moon
and the moon sees Mark
the moon is laughing
at an asteroid looking
at me

I see the moon
and the moon sees Daniel
the moon is especially full
of less testing
of our intelligence

I see the moon
and the moon sees Daniel
the moon is full of pride

I see the moon
and the moon sees Mark
the moon is full
with the bright light
of six stars

I see the moon
and the moon sees Khalil
the moon is sad
about testing his intelligence

ZACH, DYLAN, TARIN, AND DAQWHAN

A Brand New Outfit

Winter makes a chrysalis
Of snow as it turns into spring

Spring makes a chrysalis
Of butterflies as it turns into summer

Summer makes a cocoon
Of flowers as it turns into fall

Fall makes a cocoon
Of scary costumes as it turns into winter

Zach makes a cocoon of sleep
As he turns into an airplane

Dylan makes a chrysalis of wiggles
As he turns into a caterpillar

Tarin makes a cocoon of muscle
As he turns into Mr. Incredible 2

Daqwhan makes a cocoon of Daqwhan
As he turns into a werewolf

ACKNOWLEDGMENTS

B efore writing this, I think I vaguely grasped the way each book takes an entire complicated lifetime to write, but now I understand that concept with a visceral intensity (density?). And so I could (and probably should) thank everyone. (Virtually insert one hundred more pages here and yourself among them.) But in honor of the trees I will name only a few people who made my trajectory toward this book acutely possible.

I'd like to thank a handful of teachers who helped me embrace and cultivate my love of learning at every level along the way: Mary Johnson, Sheila Griffith, Greg Hewett, Susan Jaret McKinstry, Eleni Sikelianos, and André Lepecki.

And I've been endlessly lucky to learn as much from and alongside my friends as I ever did in the classroom. For the conversations, instigations, admonitions, enumerations: Colin Guthrie, Gillian Brigham, Cori Copp, Elaine Equi, Dan Machlin, Karl Krause, Simon Evans, Edmund Berrigan, Anselm Berrigan, Arlo Quint,

Christa Quint, Matt and Julie Guidry, John Coletti, Sun Yung Shin, Su Hwang, Sam Gould, Ben Polk, Sam Anders, Ted Mathys, Rachel Smith, Patrick Werle, erica kaufman, Marty Case, Shelia O'Connor, Matthew Rohrer, Emily Barbee, Serena Roth, Eric Lorberer, Tom Cox, Chris Fischbach, Daniel May, Joe Horton, Paul Austin, Jenny Austin, Brian Sufak, Aisha Sabatini Sloan, Matthew Cooperman, Brandon Brown, kari edwards, Dana Ward, Kendra Sullivan, Jared Stanley, Joanna Furman, Joseph Miller-Gamble, Farid Matuk, Susan Briante, Dan Poppick, Ashleigh Lambert, Dustin Nelson, Wren Goblirsch, Tyler Meier, Ashwini Ramaswamy, Zack Rose, Kevin Killian, Rachel Levitsky, Michael Kleber-Diggs, Matt Rasmussen, D. Allen, Roy G. Guzmán, Jeff Hansen, Elizabeth Burns, Macgregor Card, Brandon Downing, Deborah Appleman, Daniel Slager, CAConrad, Hanif Abdurraqib, Angela Pelster-Wiebe, Bryan Boyce, Alex Achen, Ben Lerner, Jenara Nerenberg, Tito Mukhopadhyay, Erin Manning, Steve Silberman, John Cary, Lara Mimosa Montes, Kao Kalia Yang, Chris Roan, Noel Black, Nick Pentzell, Danny Whitty, Rubin Hardin, Adrienne Novy, K. McClendon, Dennis Cass, Adjua Gargi Nzinga Greaves, JJJJJerome Ellis, and countless others.

A different set of thanks go to all those I've been given the grace to work for and alongside: Ryan Walquist, Sarah Marcus, Shane Endsley, Shanelle Jenkins, Daniel McSweeney, Stephen Rudin, Lorraine Anderson, Nic Kelman, Tioma Maloratsky, Marcia Eckerd, Sarah Raymont, Dustin Long, Ari Kalinowski, Allison Meek, Gerald Orange, Andy Diaz, Matt Kelly, Evan Neuwirth, Sagirah Shahid, Tijqua Daiker, and Rachel Moritz.

I give tremendous gratitude to all the organizations that Unrestricted Interest has had the honor of collaborating with: the Walker Art Center, the Minneapolis Institute of Art, Rain Taxi, the Loft Literary Center, Communities Engaging Autism, Ascendigo, the University of Arizona's Poetry Center, Carleton College, Art Resources Transfer, Spectrum Productions, The Art of Autism, *Explicit Literary Journal*, the *Brooklyn Rail*, the RCAH Center for Poetry at Michigan State University, the Poetry Project, Rumpelstiltskin Gallery, Syracuse University, the Edina Public Library, and the Walker Public Library.

And we owe a particular debt to the Autism Society of Minnesota, who have been consistent and stalwart partners from the time of our inception. I want to especially thank Dr. Barbara Luskin and Dr. Beth Pitchford, with whom I had transformational conversations, and the brilliant, ever-beaming Ellie Wilson.

A very special shout-out goes to Sallie Bernard and everyone at Ascendigo, who warmly welcomed me and Brian into their lives for a brief and deeply significant time. I feel grateful for Elizabeth Vosseller and Jason DiMambro at I-ASC and the whole Neurolyrical Café crowd, who have helped forge an unparalleled community of song and spirit. And to the teachers and administrators at the South Education Center with whom I shared the students you read about in these pages: Katie Bastiansen, Sandi Shetka, Erin Barnes, Farrah Roberson, Stephanie Hawley, Michelle Seiger, Sue Skulborstad, Cathy Pinkosky, and Jayne Tiedemann. Your classrooms are a beacon of care, trust, and joy. And to my kindred collaborators at dis assembly, who continue to welcome me deeper into neurodivergent relation and practice: Estée Klar, Jessamyn Polson, Jean Malig, Matisse ApSimon-Megens, Imane Boukaila, Adam Wolfond, Ellen Bleiwas, Ciragh Lyons, and Veronica MacLeod. And to the communication partners who also happen to be parents—Indu Eati, Estée Klar, Rachida Boukaila, Jacqueline Duby, Jennifer Bell, and Vaishnavi Sarathy—thank you for your radical hospitality, support, research, artistry, and warmth.

None of this would exist without Brian Laidlaw, who had the gentle temerity to ask me what I really wanted to do with my life. Thank you for your partnership, ease, exuberance, and creativity.

It would not exist in the same form without Lauren Russell, who challenged me to embrace my own neurodivergence unflinchingly. Thank you for always finding further ways to ask the difficult questions, quickly followed by laughter.

Early iterations of this book first appeared in *BRIGHT* magazine, *On Being, Ought: The Journal of Autistic Culture, Teaching Tolerance, Alaska Quarterly Review, Poetry Society of America, Literary Hub*, and in the forthcoming collection *Neurofutures*. I am deeply indebted to all the editors who helped these words grow, change, and find wider audiences. I owe a special debt to Sarika Bansal, who warmly welcomed the first wavering steps of this book into public life.

Many versions of this book (and thus the final version) would not exist without the interest, curiosity, insight, and critique of Susan Buckley, Miles Doyle, and Christine Ashby. My agent, Wendy Levinson, was there from the beginning until the end (and beyond!), with encouragement and savvy. Chantal Tom deftly and generously met this book where it was and made sure it was ready to meet the world. Jessie Dolch took great care with all things great and small. Mary McDermid gifted these words a quiet and superior edge where they could patiently teem. And Chiara Galimberti, how can I thank you enough for this dream of a cover?

This particular version of the book you're holding right now wouldn't exist without the friendship, intellectual labor, and emotional courage of Aviv Nisinzweig. Thank you for dancing with accountability, with joy, with discernment. I cannot imagine how I would have faced these pages, and all that they might carry, without your unrelenting brilliance.

I would not exist—in material, spiritual, or intellectual form—without my parents, Ron and Jere Martin. I never heard for one moment that who I was, how I thought, or how I moved through the world was anything less than a gift. I hope you hear in these pages how that primary acceptance allowed me to see the inherent gifts of others. Same goes for you, Courtney. I couldn't be more blessed to have you as a sister, a friend, and a mentor.

And finally, I owe everything to my wife, Mary Austin Speaker, and our two boys, Atticus and Harrison. They have supported this writing, and the work that occasioned it, in innumerable ways.

For any and all I have left out of this particular set of gratitudes, I beg your forgiveness and offer the words of Philip Whalen: "Although your name doesn't show here / I haven't forgotten you."

This book is for my students, who are also my teachers. I am so honored to be in your company and to call you my friends, my peers, my people. Let the rally continue to kiss tomorrow awake, a place where we can tilt and forge together. Let us continue to extend the choreography. Let this just be the beginning of the beginning.

NOTES

A Brief Note on Noting the Notes

I am a lover of writers and the books they write. Often in that order. These notes do not represent a thorough catalogue of writing on autism, disability, nonspeaking life, or liberation. They are a record of texts that helped move me toward better questions and extend the choreography of my own thinking during the very particular years in which I was writing this book. There are plenty of books I love dearly and might have referenced—Elizabeth Grosz's *Volatile Bodies*, Fred Moten's *In the Break*, Gaston Bachelard's *The Poetics of Space*—but they weren't on the dance card these past few years. They will be again soon, I'm sure. What I hope is that the authors I *have* mentioned here (and the works of theirs I have not mentioned) will send you cartwheeling in all directions, embracing Gwendolyn Brooks and Eli Clare and Donna Williams and countless others in turn, forever othering together.

Introduction: Keepers of the Light

1. I had originally chosen the word "jouncing" to describe Adam's movement of the stick, but he corrected me: "In the stick I want the words fasting the waves pacing the lines so the word is twallowing."

2. Here I would like to present the thinking of Erin Manning, a philosopher and artist who is also a longtime collaborator of Adam and Estée. In her book *Always More Than One: Individuation's Dance* (Duke Univ. Press, 2013), a book that explores autistic thinking and writing in great depth, she offers this resonance: "To write-with language in the making is to dance-with experience rather than exclude it from the dance" (157). Manning's deep engagement with autistic thinkers forms a kindred framework to the book you're reading now and has informed my own thinking (and dancing) in important ways.

3. To interleave Manning once more, this time from her book *The Minor Gesture* (Duke Univ. Press, 2016), "The neurotypical is the very backbone

of a concept of individuality that is absolutely divorced from the idea that relation is actually what our worlds are made of" (6).

4. Sonya Renee Taylor, *The Body Is Not an Apology: The Power of Radical Self-Love* (Berrett-Koehler, 2018), 22.

5. Having the benefit of resources like Jenara Nerenberg's *Divergent Mind: Thriving in a World That Wasn't Designed for You* (HarperOne, 2020), I can now see how "sensitive" was a code word for neurodivergent. More specifically, there now exists the acronym HSP, or highly sensitive person, denoting someone who has deeper central nervous system sensitivity, and, perhaps most relevant to my particular sensitivity, the term "emotional synesthete."

6. Hi Ellen Cooney! I survived largely undigested!

7. Neurocosmopolitan scholar Nick Walker has suggested replacing ADHD with KCS, or kinetic cognitive style, arguing that "deficit" and "disorder" reinforce a damaging pathology paradigm. I think building community around KCS has a lot of potential.

8. Only playing basketball had a similar effect, matching my intrinsic love of the game with an optimal level of challenge. Unfortunately, the flow I felt on the court was repeatedly fractured by the casual and often violent abuse I found in locker rooms, not to mention the seemingly endless stream of homophobic and misogynist bluster.

9. And of course there are literal restraints at work as well, highlighted by the recent controversy over a film portraying an autistic individual subjected to prone restraint, a method that has not only traumatized many in the autistic community, but led to the deaths of autistic people. In response to this controversy, CommunicationFirst, working with nonspeaking autistic writers, produced a short film called *LISTEN* that I highly recommend: https://communicationfirst.org/LISTEN/.

10. In 2021, Max began to self-identify as nonbinary. Before that time, their publications bore the name Chetan Junnuru, and they used masculine pronouns. Max's journey in this regard was paralleled by his sibling Mark, who began to self-identify with masculine pronouns in 2021. Before that time, his publications bore the name Meghana Junnuru, and he used feminine pronouns. All three of us would have loved to include this story of transition and self-identification in this book, but agreed that it would benefit from more time and care than the publication timeline would allow.

11. The modes of AAC are about as varied as the people they serve. We all use forms of AAC throughout our day, whether it's reading facial expressions or taking notes on our phones. More than two dozen conditions and disabilities make direct speech an unreliable form of communication, and AACs—anything from the physiological support of a communication part-

ner to a computer voice synthesizer to sign language—have proved to help tremendously.

12. Kamila Markram and Henry Markram, "The Intense World Theory—A Unifying Theory of the Neurobiology of Autism," *Frontiers in Human Neuroscience*, December 21, 2010, https://www.frontiersin.org/articles/10.3389/fnhum.2010.00224/full. A useful profile of the Markrams by Maia Szalavitz can be found at https://medium.com/matter/the-boy-whose-brain-could-unlock-autism-70c3d64ff221, "The Boy Whose Brain Could Unlock Autism," Medium, Matter, December 11, 2013.

13. Audre Lorde, *Sister Outsider* (Penguin, 2020), 25. The quoted passage is from Lorde's short masterpiece "Poetry Is Not a Luxury," which forms a breathtaking distillation of so much that this book endeavors to say and do.

14. For more radical and poetic insights like this, please explore the incomparable podcast brown shares with her sister, Autumn: *How to Survive the End of the World*.

15. In this spirit, I want to draw your attention to just a few groundbreaking collections of writing that articulate the variousness of disabled life: *Beauty Is a Verb: The New Poetry of Disability*, ed. Sheila Black, Jennifer Bartlett, and Michael Northen (Cinco Puntos, 2011); *All the Weight of Our Dreams: On Living Racialized Autism*, ed. Lydia X. Z. Brown, E. Ashkenazy, and Morénike Giwa Onaiwu (DragonBee, 2017); and *Disability Visibility: First-Person Stories from the Twenty-First Century*, ed. Alice Wong (Vintage, 2020).

16. Manning, *Always More Than One*, 183.

17. This is an excerpt from a forthcoming book of prose.

Chapter 1: Like Water I Am Eager

1. Which doesn't mean it wasn't also akin to torture. They were gently forcing Mark, all day long, to answer questions that he had no motivation to answer in a manner that did not accommodate his sensorimotor needs.

2. See his memoir, *Born on a Blue Day: Inside the Extraordinary Mind of an Autistic Savant* (Free Press, 2007).

3. *Autism: The Movement Sensing Perspective*, ed. Elizabeth B. Torres and Caroline Whyatt (CRC Press, 2017), 3.

4. Torres and Whyatt, *Autism*, xv.

5. M. Remi Yergeau, *Authoring Autism: On Rhetoric and Neurological Queerness* (Duke Univ. Press, 2018), 7.

6. Personal correspondence with the author, September 22, 2020. Woolgar adds: "So far, we've been hampered in two major ways. First, there has

been a general reluctance to include nonspeakers in research because they are seen as difficult to test. Second, most of our scientific tests depend on the participant being able to give meaningful motor responses. This means that ability to understand is conflated with the ability to coordinate and carry out the motor actions needed to respond. If I ask you to 'point to the picture of a dog,' you have to both understand what I'm wanting you to do (language comprehension) and be able to coordinate your bodily movements to do it (motor action). If either of these are difficult for a person, they will score poorly, and we won't know why."

7. Julia Miele Rodas, *Autistic Disturbances: Theorizing Autism Poetics from the DSM to Robinson Crusoe* (Univ. of Michigan Press, 2018), 73.

8. Rodas, *Autistic Disturbances*, 5.

9. And anyone who has had the indelible experience of viewing Mel Baggs's groundbreaking 2007 video work *In My Language* knows that these "native languages" encompass far more than words. Baggs writes: "My language is not about designing words or even visual symbols for people to interpret. It is about being in a constant conversation with every aspect of my environment. Reacting physically to all parts of my surroundings" (https://www.youtube.com/watch?v=JnylM1hI2jc).

10. Rodas, *Autistic Disturbances*, 2.

11. This comes to me by way of Brandon Brown's *Top 40* (Roof Books, 2014), in which he quotes David Brazil quoting Angela Davis speaking on the first day of Oakland's 2011 General Strike.

12. Dara McAnulty, *Diary of a Young Naturalist* (Milkweed Editions, 2021), 130.

13. This passion is also an echo of adrienne maree brown's insistence on "positive obsession" at the core of an activist life, which is itself an echo of Octavia Butler, who wrote in *Parable of the Sower*, "Prodigy is, at its essence, adaptability and persistent, positive obsession. . . . Without positive obsession, there is nothing at all."

14. Having perceived this in autistic writing from my very first experience of working with neurodivergent students, I was ecstatic the first time I saw it borne out in scholarly terms by Ralph James Savarese in his essay "The Lobes of Autobiography: Poetry and Autism," which was published by *Stone Canoe* in 2008. Savarese continues to deepen his investigation into the autistic and the poetic. His most recent book, *See It Feelingly: Classic Novels, Autistic Readers, and the Schooling of a No-Good English Professor* (Duke Univ. Press, 2018), takes an especially detailed look at autistic modes of reading.

15. I recently asked Adam about these vocalizations, and he wrote that these "hums" are his way of "annotating the way I need to move like the marginalia of expression." He added that they are his alternative to the way

"fast talkers," with changes in pitch or inflection, seamlessly add emotional marginalia to their own spoken language, "buttressing human hums that annotate the life of words." I can't help but grow giddy humming Adam's words into their own annotation here.

Chapter 2: A Place Where the Islands Touch

1. Researchers like Penny Spikins at the University of York have been tracking the ways in which the origins of art and autism might indeed be related: see Penny Spikins, "Did Autism Help Drive Human Evolution?," *Wired*, April 4, 2017, https://www.wired.co.uk/article/autism-ancestors-evolution.

2. Some research is even pointing to a link between autistic synesthesia and savant abilities in math and language: see Andreas Riedel, Simon Maier, Kerstin Wenzler, Bernd Feige, Ludger Tebartz van Else, Sven Bölte, and Janina Neufel, "A Case of Co-Occurring Synesthesia, Autism, Prodigious Talent and Strong Structural Brain Connectivity," *BMC Psychiatry* 20, 342 (2020), https://doi.org/10.1186/s12888-020-02722-w.

3. Writer and brain scientist V. S. Ramachandran has written at length about this connection of synesthesia, metaphor, and autism, and although I find his work fascinating, I have not included it here because I also find it to be neuroreductive and, frankly, condescending in its relation to autistic experience.

4. I first discovered this phrasing in Chardin's *Hymn of the Universe* (1974), which I bought because of its gorgeous cover. Another text I find very useful when thinking of the purpose and origins of language is Steven Mithen's *The Singing Neanderthals: The Origins of Music, Language, Mind and Body* (2005), which posits song as the proto-language for which we've long been searching. Since I understand song and poetry to share the same root, this reinforces my belief that poetry is a fundamental aspect of human experience.

5. Manning, *Minor Gesture*, 15.

6. "'We Need Much Better Standards of Research in Autism Intervention': An Interview with Dr. Damian Milton," *Noncompliant—The Podcast*, January 4, 2020, https://noncompliantpodcast.com/2020/01/04/we-need-much-better-standards-of-research-in-autism-intervention-an-interview-with-dr-damian-milton/.

7. Adam Smith, "The Empathy Imbalance Hypothesis of Autism: A Theoretical Approach to Cognitive and Emotional Empathy in Autistic Development," *Psychological Record* 59 (July 2009): 489–510, https://doi.org/10.1007/BF03395675.

8. The original interview, "More Than a Thing to Ignore: An Interview with Tito Rajarshi Mukhopadhyay," appeared in *Disability Studies Quarterly* 30,

no. 1 (2010). A further article exploring this question at length, "I Object: Autism, Empathy, and the Trope of Personification," is available as a talk Savarese gave at Emory University: https://www.youtube.com/watch?v=uZxfeA8thjc.

9. Tito Mukhopadhyay, *Plankton Dreams* (Open Humanities, 2015), 8.

10. Alexis Pauline Gumbs, *Undrowned: Black Feminist Lessons from Marine Mammals* (AK Press, 2020), 32.

11. I'm thinking of Elijah McClain and Laquan McDonald, though there are countless told and untold. It's important to note that even the life of a care worker like Charles Kinsey can be imperiled if, in attempting to protect their friend, they move at the pace of autism.

12. The simple answer, of course, is consequences, but there are countless neurodivergent individuals whose bodies and minds preclude them from fulfilling the expectations of the social trap, even if they somehow wanted to.

13. The events I'm writing about here predate the merging of Asperger syndrome and autism spectrum disorder in the DSM-5.

Chapter 3: The Moon Is Especially Full

1. Tito Mukhopadhyay, *The Mind Tree: A Miraculous Child Breaks the Silence of Autism* (Arcade, 2003), 80–81.

2. An excerpt from Adam's forthcoming book of prose.

3. Not only is this one of my favorite films, documentary or otherwise, but I was able to present it to a crowd at the Bryant Lake Bowl and Theater in Minneapolis, alongside Mark Eati and his teacher Katie Bastiansen, as part of the Writers Go to the Movies Series in 2018.

4. From a short essay found in the groundbreaking anthology *Leaders Around Me: Autobiographies of Autistics Who Type, Point, & Spell to Communicate*, ed. Edlyn Vallejo Peña (2019). For a rich exploration of Bissonnette's writing, see the essay "Gobs and Gobs of Metaphor: Dynamic Relation and a Classical Autist's Typed Massage," by Ralph James Savarese, which can be downloaded from Inflexions at https://www.inflexions.org/n5_t _Savarese.pdf.

Chapter 4: The Listening World

1. McAnulty, *Diary of a Young Naturalist*, 25.

2. David Abram, *The Spell of the Sensuous: Perception and Language in a More-Than-Human World* (Vintage, 1997), 9.

3. Abram, *Spell of the Sensuous*, 9.

4. Though she hasn't rejected factory farming outright, Grandin's work as an industrial designer and theorist of slaughterhouse machinery has made the deaths of innumerable cows less cruel, and she has lately shifted her focus toward smaller and more inherently humane farming operations. And yet, one still can't escape the fact that she has given the meat industry an ethical cover. It's complicated, to say the least.

5. Aarti Nair, Morgan Jolliffe, Yong Seuk S. Lograsso, and Carrie E. Bearden, "A Review of Default Mode Network Connectivity and Its Association with Social Cognition in Adolescents with Autism Spectrum Disorder and Early-Onset Psychosis," *Frontiers in Psychiatry*, June 25, 2020, https://www.frontiersin.org/article/10.3389/fpsyt.2020.00614.

6. Gonzalo Bénard, "An Autistic Shaman Shares Why Autistic People Make Good Shamans," The Art of Autism, September 5, 2018, https://the-art-of-autism.com/an-autistic-shaman-shares-why-autistic-people-make-good-shamans/.

7. Sunaura Taylor, *Beasts of Burden: Animal and Disability Liberation* (New Press, 2017), 120–121. I couldn't recommend this book more highly. Taylor's thorough thought-making around animal and disability justice, rooted in her own experience as a disabled artist, is as nourishing as it is harrowing. It is also an ideal place to explore the conundrum of Temple Grandin cited above.

8. Erin Manning and Brian Massumi, *Thought in the Act: Passages in the Ecology of Experience* (Univ. of Minnesota Press, 2014), 6.

9. Robin Wall Kimmerer, *Braiding Sweetgrass: Indigenous Wisdom, Scientific Knowledge, and the Teaching of Plants* (Milkweed Editions, 2013), 372.

Chapter 5: A Brand New Outfit

1. Yergeau, *Authoring Autism*, 43.

2. Hilde M. Geurts, Blythe Corbett, and Marjorie Solomon, "The Paradox of Cognitive Flexibility in Autism," *Trends in Cognitive Science* 13, no. 2 (2009): 74–82, https://www.ncbi.nlm.nih.gov/pmc/articles/PMC5538880/.

3. Barry M. Prizant, *Uniquely Human: A Different Way of Seeing Autism* (Simon & Schuster, 2015), 84.

4. Gwen Westerman and Bruce White, *Mni Sota Makoce: The Land of the Dakota* (Minnesota Historical Society Press, 2012).

5. McAnulty, *Diary of a Young Naturalist*, 23–24.

Chapter 6: I Can Be My Real Self

1. Specifically the iteration of Courteney Cox from her breakout role in *Ace Ventura: Pet Detective.*

2. John F. Strang, Lauren Kenworthy, Aleksandra Dominska, et al., "Increased Gender Variance in Autism Spectrum Disorders and Attention Deficit Hyperactivity Disorder," *Archives of Sexual Behavior* 43, no. 8 (2014): 1525–1533, doi:10.1007/s10508-014-0285-3.

3. Yergeau provides a helpful gloss of the term "neuroqueer" and its origins in *Authoring Autism*, 26–27.

4. Nick Walker, "Neuroqueer: An Introduction," 2015, last updated 2021, https://neuroqueer.com/neuroqueer-an-introduction/.

5. See, for example, Alex Kronstein, "Treating Autism as a Problem: The Connection Between Gay Conversion Therapy and ABA," Nova Scotia Advocate, July 11, 2018, https://nsadvocate.org/2018/07/11/treating-autism-as-a-problem-the-connection-between-gay-conversion-therapy-and-aba/; Elizabeth DeVita-Raeburn and Spectrum, "Is the Most Common Therapy for Autism Cruel?," *The Atlantic*, August 11, 2016, https://www.theatlantic.com/health/archive/2016/08/aba-autism-controversy/495272/; and Elizabeth DeVita-Raeburn, "The Controversy over Autism's Most Common Therapy," Spectrum, August 10, 2016, https://www.spectrumnews.org/features/deep-dive/controversy-autisms-common-therapy/.

6. "Autistic Self-Advocacy Network, LGBT Groups Release Statement of Needs of Trans Autistic People," ASAN, June 22, 2016, https://autisticadvocacy.org/2016/06/autistic-self-advocacy-network-lgbt-groups-release-statement-on-needs-of-trans-autistic-people/.

Chapter 7: Becoming Rainbow Man

1. From DJ Savarese, *A Doorknob for the Eye*, available at http://www.djsavarese.com/3d-flip-book/doorknobfortheeye/.

Chapter 8: Living in a State of Hell

1. This concept is explored in great depth by Resmaa Menakem in his book *My Grandmother's Hands: Racialized Trauma and the Pathway to Mending Our Hearts and Minds* (Central Recovery Press, 2017).

2. Living white in America can also be a kind of hell, rife with spiritual disfigurement and often compounding its deformations by masquerading as heaven.

3. A useful discussion of standpoint theory and how it relates to intersectionality can be found in an episode of *Scene on Radio*, "S3 E4: Feminism in Black and White," August 22, 2018, https://www.sceneonradio.org/episode-50-feminism-in-black-and-white-men-part-4/.

4. Diane di Prima, "Revolutionary Letter #10", in *Revolutionary Letters* (City Lights Books, 1971), 19.

5. "Junauda Petrus Reads Her Poem: Give the Police Departments to the Grandmothers," Vimeo, https://vimeo.com/426276718.

Chapter 9: Calm-Arriving to a Wanting Safe World

1. Or, as Jessi Dolch pointed out to me, you might also encounter billowing, in its proper context, while reading The Book of Psalms. She wrote: "I'm not a Christian, but Psalm 42 is a lovely one about grief and hope and comfort, with the lines 'Deep calls to deep / at the thunder of your cataracts; / all your waves and your billows / have gone over me.' This also came to me as I read this poem."

2. Lorde, *Sister Outsider*, 102.

3. I came to Neil Marcus's work by way of Sunaura Taylor, who cites the quotation here as featured in *Occupying Disability: Critical Approaches to Community, Justice, and Decolonizing Disability*, ed. Pamela Block, Devva Kasnitz, Akemi Nishida, and Nick Pollard (Springer, 2015).

Chapter 10: The How of Autism

1. "COVID 19 Artist Feature Five: Imane Boukaila," April 26, 2020, https://explicitliteraryjournal.com/2020/04/26/covid-19-feature-five-imane-boukaila/.

2. For a thorough examination of this topic, see Torres and Whyatt, *Autism*, or download a digital version at https://www.researchgate.net/publication/316954991_Autism_The_Movement_Sensing_Perspective.

3. Often readers discover this work in our newsletter, The Listening World, which can be found at thelisteningworld.substack.com.

4. See adrienne maree brown's theory that all political organizing is an act of science fiction, which she describes in *Pleasure Activism: The Politics of Feeling Good* (AK Press, 2019) as "shaping the future we long for and have not yet experienced" (10).

5. Rodas, *Autistic Disturbances*, 9–10.

6. Also from Manning, *Always More Than One*: "the *how* of knowing much exceeds the *what* (and the who) of knowing" (181).

7. Lorde, *Sister Outsider*, 42.

8. brown, *Pleasure Activism*, 50.

9. Yergeau, *Authoring Autism*, 27.

Chapter 11: May Today Be Awake

1. Mukhopadhyay, *Mind Tree*, 117.

2. I do also want to note, however, how much joy Sid takes in refusing simplicity, an act of resistance I hear alongside Alexis Pauline Gumbs, who writes about honoring "what it means to refuse to be seen, to be known, to participate when politics as we know them have prioritized recognition by and access to the dominant paradigm." Gumbs goes on to praise "all those who love with a depth beyond recognition, nurturing freedom over understandability, valuing life as so much more than simple comprehension" (*Undrowned*, 109–110).

3. "2017 Poems and Art for Peace Blog 2," The Art of Autism, September 1, 2017, https://the-art-of-autism.com/2017-poems-and-art-for-peace-blog-2/.

4. "May Poem," August 1, 2017, http://growourjoy.org/2017/08/01/may/.

Coda: Full Spiral

1. Although Max's name is the only one to appear on the cover, and they indeed did write many of the poems on their own, the chapbook features many collaborations with Mark, who also played a role in helping Max edit the chapbook.

2. Unrestricted Interest is an LLC. That may change, but thus far it's suited our poets' ways, making what we can in the time we glean between raising kids, climbing mountains, playing gigs, and writing our own poems.

Afterword: Belonging to the Future

1. Which gives them no less a legal claim to the land than those who view it as property. In addition to their historical claim, the Dakota people's ethic of stewardship and relation gives them a superior moral claim as well. For more on this topic, I highly recommend Martin Case's unparalleled exploration *The Relentless Business of Treaties: How Indigenous Land Became U.S. Property* (Minnesota Historical Society Press, 2018).

2. That said, my family does possess the indenture of my great-great-grandfather Edward Chapman, an Irishman who, by way of temporary servitude, settled down with his Scottish wife, Isabella Meldrum, in late-nineteenth-century Nebraska. Chapman comes from the profession of the chapman, a peddler of cheap goods. This is where the term "chapbook" arises, the chapman selling small, cheap volumes on the street. So I come from the distribution and democratization of literature as well.

3. Mohawk seed keeper Rowen White speaks of diaspora as a nearly universal experience and how each of us has been born into the grief of displacement, severed from the roots of our indigenous knowing. She also points toward a diaspora of language, enacted brutally among indigenous people by forced boarding schools where native languages were forbidden. Both Hannah and I feel a distinct diasporic breach between us and the wild language of our Celtic ancestors, something we've discussed at length. I first heard White speak of these topics on Prentis Hemphill's *Finding Our Way* podcast, in an episode titled "Seeds, Grief, and Memory with Rowen White."

4. Like so many disabled individuals before us, my mother and I have learned a thousand ways to better sustain ourselves with care, ingenuity, and resilience. I am grateful every day for her mentorship and grieve that she had to face the disequilibrium of disability unmentored for so many years.

5. Gumbs, *Undrowned*, 8.

6. These gifts allow me to sense minute changes in the emotional tenor of others, which is a crucial aspect of my work; but they often backfire at home, where parenting small children whose emotional landscape changes minute by minute can whiplash my nervous system until I'm facedown on the carpet.

7. I can spot animals in a field or remember exactly where my wife left her keys but am also constantly reorganizing spaces since an unintentional clutter leaves me addled. In my house we talk often of where things belong, and I can't help but see each object—cup, rock, book, pen—as a subject seeking to find its place.

8. *Care Work* (Arsenal Pulp Press, 2019) is a crucial resource guide for what it has meant to be intersectionally disabled over the past half century and what it might mean moving forward. It's one of the clearest and most vibrant examples I know for articulating the ways in which queer, neurodivergent, BIPOC (Black, indigenous, and people of color), and disabled artists have created ingenious, community-based responses to the problems of our current society.